The American Poets Project
is published with a gift in memory of
JAMES MERRILL

Edna St. Vincent Millay

selected poems

j. d. m^cclatchy editor

AMERICAN POETS PROJECT

THE LIBRARY OF AMERICA

Published in the United States by Library of America.
Visit our website at www.loa.org.

This paper meets the requirements of ANSI / NISO Z39.48–1992 (Permanence of Paper).

Design by Chip Kidd and Mark Melnick.
Frontispiece photo by Berenice Abbott.

Library of Congress Cataloging-in-Publication Data:
Millay, Edna St. Vincent, 1892–1950
[Poems. Selections]
Selected poems / Edna St. Vincent Millay ; J.D. McClatchy, editor
p. cm. — (American poets project ; 1)
Includes index.
ISBN 978–1–931082–35–8 (alk. paper)
I. Title: Edna St. Vincent Millay. II. McClatchy, J.D., 1945- III. Title. IV. Series
PS3525.I495 A6 2003
811´.52 — dc2
2002032126
10 9 8 7 6 5 4 3

Edna
St. Vincent
Millay

CONTENTS

Introduction   xvii

I

from *Renascence and Other Poems* (1917)

    Renascence   3
    Interim   10
    Afternoon on a Hill   18
    Witch-Wife   18
    When the Year Grows Old   19
    "Time does not bring relief; you all have lied"   20
    "If I should learn, in some quite casual way"   21
    Bluebeard   22

from *A Few Figs from Thistles* (1920)

    First Fig   23
    Second Fig   23
    Recuerdo   23
    To the Not Impossible Him   24
    Grown-up   25
    Daphne   25
    Midnight Oil   25

The Philosopher   26

"I think I should have loved you presently"   26

"I shall forget you presently, my dear"   27

from *Second April* (1921)

Eel-Grass   28

Elegy Before Death   28

Weeds   29

Passer Mortuus Est   30

Alms   30

Inland   31

Ebb   32

from Memorial to D. C.

    I. Epitaph   33

    IV. Dirge   33

    V. Elegy   34

"Only until this cigarette is ended"   35

"Once more into my arid days like dew"   36

"When I too long have looked upon your face"   36

"And you as well must die, belovèd dust"   37

"As to some lovely temple, tenantless"   38

Wild Swans   38

from *The Harp-Weaver and Other Poems* (1923)

Autumn Chant   39

Feast   40

The Betrothal   40

The Ballad of the Harp-Weaver   41

Never May the Fruit Be Plucked   46

Hyacinth   47

To One Who Might Have Borne a Message   47

"Love is not blind. I see with single eye"   48

"Pity me not because the light of day"   48

"Here is a wound that never will heal, I know"   49

"Your face is like a chamber where a king"   50

"I, being born a woman and distressed"   50

"What lips my lips have kissed, and where, and why"   51
"How healthily their feet upon the floor"   51
"Euclid alone has looked on Beauty bare"   52
Sonnets from an Ungrafted Tree   53

from *The Buck in the Snow* (1928)
To the Wife of a Sick Friend   63
To a Friend Estranged from Me   64
The Buck in the Snow   65
Evening on Lesbos   65
Dirge Without Music   66
Lethe   67
To Inez Milholland   68
To Jesus on His Birthday   68
"Not that it matters, not that my heart's cry"   69

II
Aria da Capo (1921)   73
from *The King's Henchman* (1927)
Ælfrida's Song   97
Love Scene   99
Translations from *Flowers of Evil*
by Charles Baudelaire (1936)
The Fang   105
Parisian Dream   106
Invitation to the Voyage   108
The Old Servant   110
Late January   111
The King of the Rainy Country   111
Mists and Rains   112
A Memory   113

III
Fatal Interview (1931)   117

IV

from *Wine from These Grapes* (1934)

    Valentine   **147**

    In the Grave No Flower   **147**

    Childhood Is the Kingdom Where Nobody Dies   **148**

    The Solid Sprite Who Stands Alone   **150**

    Spring in the Garden   **151**

    Sonnet ("Time, that renews the tissues of this frame")   **152**

    Desolation Dreamed Of   **152**

    On the Wide Heath   **153**

    Two Sonnets in Memory   **154**

    Conscientious Objector   **155**

    Epitaph for the Race of Man   **156**

from *Conversation at Midnight* (1937)

    "Thus are our altars polluted; nor may we flee. . . ."   **166**

    "The mind thrust out of doors"   **172**

from *Huntsman, What Quarry?* (1939)

    The Snow Storm   **174**

    Not So Far as the Forest   **174**

    "Fontaine, Je Ne Boirai Pas De Ton Eau!"   **177**

    The True Encounter   **178**

    Czecho-Slovakia   **178**

    Underground System   **179**

    Two Voices   **180**

    This Dusky Faith   **181**

    To a Young Poet   **182**

    To Elinor Wylie   **182**

    "Now that the west is washed of clouds and clear"   **186**

    "I too beneath your moon, almighty Sex"   **187**

    "Thou famished grave, I will not fill thee yet"   **187**

    "Not only love plus awful grief"   **188**

from *Make Bright the Arrows* (1940)

    "Make bright the arrows"   **189**

    An Eclipse of the Sun Is Predicted   **189**

"Gentlemen Cry, Peace!" 190

"I must not die of pity; I must live" 191

from *The Murder of Lidice* (1942)

"They marched them out to the public square" 192

from *Mine the Harvest* (1954)

Small Hands, Relinquish All 195

Ragged Island 196

"To whom the house of Montagu" 197

"The courage that my mother had" 199

Armenonville 199

Dream of Saba 200

For Warmth Alone, for Shelter Only 204

"Black hair you'd say she had, or rather" 204

Steepletop 206

"Look how the bittersweet with lazy muscle
 moves aside" 207

"Those hours when happy hours were my estate" 209

"Not to me, less lavish—though my dreams have
 been splendid" 209

"Tranquility at length, when autumn comes" 210

Sonnet in Dialectic 210

"It is the fashion now to wave aside" 211

"Admetus, from my marrow's core I do" 212

"I will put Chaos into fourteen lines" 212

"And must I then, indeed, Pain, live with you" 213

"Felicity of Grief!—even Death being kind" 213

"If I die solvent—die, that is to say" 214

Biographical Note 217

Note on the Texts 218

Notes 220

Index of Titles and First Lines 223

INTRODUCTION

If literary historians can agree on anything, it's that the road to hell is often paved with good reviews. At the start of her career, Edna St. Vincent Millay's reviews were astonishing. By 1912, when she was just eighteen, she was already famous. When, five years later, her first book appeared, she was launched on a rushing current of acclaim. If by the end of her life most of the good reviews were merely dutiful, for the run of years in between—during the tumultuous decades of the '20s and '30s, in a world between wars, at first jazzed and roaring, later impoverished and threatened—her readers and critics clung to her celebrity and swooned over her poems. Even so severe a reader as A. E. Housman praised her virtuosity. Thomas Hardy once famously said that the two great things about America were its skyscrapers and the poetry of Edna St. Vincent Millay. In 1952, two years after her death, when it was already unfashionable to admire Millay, her devoted reader and one-time lover Edmund Wilson insisted that "Edna Millay seems to me one of the only poets writing in English in our time who have attained to anything like the stature of the great literary figures." But that was the last time such a claim was made. By 1976, she was not even represented in *The New Oxford Book of American Verse*. The sand had all run through the hourglass. How changed everything was from the beginning, when Millay, still a student at Vassar, first dazzled Manhattan's literary salons. She looked like a candle: small, intense, pale, with hair the color of fire. And in a voice surprisingly deep and exquisitely controlled, she would read her latest poem. Louis Untermeyer was there and remembered that "there was no other voice like hers in America. It was the sound of the ax on fresh wood."

So what happened? Millay herself, in a letter, once blamed the decline of her reputation on her political activism. In fact, she had eloquently championed Sacco and Vanzetti in 1927, and a decade later vigorously campaigned against American isolationism. And throughout her career she was an ardent feminist. All this made her a prominent target for the disapproval of some. Though her propaganda work during the war taxed her always fragile health and neurotic temperament, and she herself realized that her poems of this period were inferior to her best, this can hardly have been the only reason for the decline in her critical stature. It is more likely that the alcohol and drug addiction that plagued the last fifteen years of her life drained her powers of concentration, though her posthumous collection, *Mine the Harvest*, contains poems as fleetingly spirited as before. All along, of course, there had been sniping, some of it from those suspicious that her celebrity had inflated her literary reputation, and some from the male critical establishment which had long since bought up the shares in T. S. Eliot's Modernism, Inc. In a 1937 essay, for instance, John Crowe Ransom described Millay as "the best of the poets who are 'popular' and loved by Circles, Leagues, Lyceums, and Round Tables," and went on to complain that she is "fixed in her famous attitudes, and is indifferent to intellectuality." He says that because, after all, "a woman lives for love," and "man distinguishes himself from woman by intellect." This defines her limitation:

> If I must express it in a word, I feel still obliged to say it is her lack of intellectual interest. It is that which the male reader misses in her poetry, even though he may acknowledge the authenticity of the interest which is there. I used a conventional symbol, which I hope was not objectionable, when I phrased this lack of hers: deficiency in masculinity.

Opinions like that nearly take the breath away now, but in fact Ransom's kind of venomous condescension has echoed down the years. The terms of contempt may have shifted, but the intention has been constant: to ridicule Millay's haplessly old-fashioned manner and the shallowness of her sensibility. The fact that, during this same time, young readers, especially women, kept making their secret discoveries of Millay's sway over their hearts mattered little. Critical opinion had blown out the flame.

It is an odd irony that her detractors, even today, dismiss her work as sentimental, cloying, fusty. In their day, of course, her poems startled readers with their edgy candor, their fearless passion, their silvery structures. This only points up the shifting tides of cultural assumptions, and should serve to remind us how incautious have been more recent evaluations of her achievement. Take as an example one of her earliest and best-known sonnets:

> If I should learn, in some quite casual way,
> That you were gone, not to return again—

Read from the back-page of a paper, say,
Held by a neighbor in a subway train,
How at the corner of this avenue
And such a street (so are the papers filled)
A hurrying man, who happened to be you,
At noon today had happened to be killed—
I should not cry aloud—I could not cry
Aloud, or wring my hands in such a place—
I should but watch the station lights rush by
With a more careful interest on my face;
Or raise my eyes and read with greater care
Where to store furs and how to treat the hair.

The poem was published in 1917, as part of her first book, *Renascence*. It is, first of all, a remarkably adroit sonnet, its single sentence unfurling across the octet's premise and the sestet's conclusion. It takes up the sonnet's traditional subject matter—the conjunction of love and mortality—and gives it an unusual setting, and a modern tone. The voice is pitched at a conversational level—you hear the poem *spoken*. Its casual address moves fluently through the form's corridors. And still, it's what is not said that is most eloquent. The sudden churning emotion of the speaker's horrified discovery—as accidental as the death of her beloved itself—is choked back unspoken, suppressed. The advertisements she concentrates on—like the newspaper item she has just seen, a slice of modern life—have, of course, the air of the mortuary about them. And the dramatic effect of the whole poem depends on the images, at once startling and ordinary, in that eerie last line. (It was characteristic of Millay to open a sonnet abruptly and close it with a calculatedly arresting last line. Thornton Wilder, quoting a great sonneteer, once remarked that "one line in fourteen comes from the ceiling; the others have to be adjusted around it." Millay's last lines are from the ceiling.)

But what I want to draw attention to is not the poem's artistry but its date. The poem is set in a subway, a trench of sorts. And in 1917 the trenches of France were on everyone's mind. English poets like Wilfred Owen and Siegfried Sassoon were writing the poems of death, but the bitter ironies in their poems were gargantuan and grotesque. Millay's sonnet might be read as a war poem, if its oncoming automobile had been, say, a grenade. Instead, it poses as a realistic account of a chance accident and its immediate aftermath. But the intimacy of Millay's rendering, its psychological acuity, lifts it above its occasion. And what poet, in 1917, was writing with this sort of brutal and elegant immediacy? Whose sense of irony was as stinging? In 1927, in one of the very first profiles to run in *The New Yorker*, Griffin Barry (also a former lover) wrote of overhearing American strangers in Paris cafés in 1921 already reciting Millay's love sonnets by heart.

Apparently, at least, one section of the incoming generation had seen nothing so accurate about itself in print. Consider the time: we had just gone into the war, and a roll-call in the camp of American letters would have brought up a hundred explorers of the social problems to one of love. . . . The jazz age was unknown. Fitzgerald had yet to write his descriptions of moneyed, jigging youth. Dos Passos had not uttered the contempt with which sensitive youth saw the war, nor the wildness that followed when he got back home. The war itself had barely begun. The war passed over us in thunder. . . . At the end, sonnets by a girl in Greenwich Village about "fierce and trivial love" began to be widely known. . . . Her public cohered quickly in 1919 when the boys got back from France—boys fresh from the wars, hungrily fierce about love and as trivial as you please and the young women of the day became fierce and trivial, too. It is not an easy way of life for women—not always. The young women needed a poet. Edna Millay became that one, hardly aware of it herself, at first.

Women had never written such poems. There is a tone of defiance, of smiling contempt, in some of her sonnets about the war between the sexes that readers in the '20s would have thrilled to, and readers today are still intrigued by:

> I know my mind and I have made my choice;
> Not from your temper does my doom depend;
> Love me or love me not, you have no voice
> In this, which is my portion to the end. . . .
> Here might you bless me; what you cannot do
> Is bow me down, who have been loved by you.

Elsewhere, as when she writes that "the bankrupt heart is free," there is a bracing insouciance. Its rueful wit is lined with dark silk:

> Well, I have lost you; and I lost you fairly;
> In my own way, and with my full consent.
> Say what you will, kings in a tumbrel rarely
> Went to their deaths more proud than this one went.

In the living room at Steepletop, the home she shared with her husband in rural New York, Millay kept a bronze bust of Sappho. It was the appropriate household god. Until Millay, few women poets since Sappho had written so explicitly of passion, whether of its erotic bonds or of its emotional writhings. But it was less passion itself than her perspectives on it that give her poems their distinctive tone. Above all, she was a romantic ironist. The final couplet of one sonnet phrases the disparity perfectly:

> Pity me that the heart is slow to learn
> What the swift mind beholds at every turn.

The slow heart and the swift mind are the instruments of our undoing, and art does not side with either. Millay's dramatization of desire's knotted toils and of understanding's cold comforts remains a remarkable achievement. But behind it looms a huge shadow. The engine that drove her poetry—as it may have propelled her life, through love affairs and addictions—was death. Her fear of it haunted her desperate apostrophes to the romantic moment, and chilled her appraisals of loss. The title poem of her last book, published from beyond the grave, describes a garden, its brilliant colors "striped with black, the tulip, lawn, and vine, / Like gardens looked at through an iron gate." Mortality is the prison of our days, and its force echoes through all of Millay's work. Her very first success, "Renascence," is a visionary account of being buried alive—a spiritual death described as a grave from which she can still sense the world, the rain seeping down, the invisible sunlight above: "How can I bear it, buried here, / While overhead the sky grows clear / And blue again after the storm?" In her verse-play, *Aria da Capo*, written and performed directly after the Great War, death is invited to the feast, and it hovers menacingly over everything afterward.

■

Born in 1892 on the coast of Maine, Edna St. Vincent Millay grew up acting. Her parents had divorced; her father decamped, and her mother, a visiting nurse and itinerant hairweaver, was usually on the road. The three Millay girls—Edna, the eldest, Norma, and Kathleen, all born within four years—were left on their own, each assigned tasks they made into games. It was a pinched and lonely childhood, and prompted Millay to create in her diary imaginary parents and friends, romantic figures representing the security she lacked and the escape she longed for. Childhood make-believe turned into local theatricals, and Millay acted and even toured as a girl; still later, at Vassar, she wrote and starred in the school plays, and eventually studied acting seriously. From the start, she was eager to put over her lines, to work for applause. And there is something theatrical at the heart of her work. In this, as in much else, she resembles Lord Byron, who made himself into a glamorous and rakish character and then wrote about that character as if he were writing about himself. Behind the flamboyant self-presentation is a quieter, less certain autobiography—the small, sweating actress inside the heavy lion costume.

Even as a child, she was a voracious reader and, encouraged by her mother, she steeped herself in Shakespeare, Tennyson, Wordsworth, Longfellow, Keats, and Shelley. She started a novel at the age of eight, and at sixteen she carefully wrote out dozens of poems in a brown copybook and presented to her mother the "Poetical Works of Vincent Millay." The Romantic and Victorian poets transfixed her young imagination, and guided it until the end. Later in life, she would dazzle visitors by reciting from memory whole anthologies—not just Wordsworth or Shelley or Hopkins, but Dante and Petrarch, Racine and Heine. What was in her head was also in her pen. I suspect it is her diction that gives many readers pause these days—too many abstractions and inversions, too much *I pray you* and *thou canst not*. This affects the sonnets especially. Sonnets were a highlight of Millay's first book, and of most every volume that followed. She usually grouped them at the end of the book, knowing they were what was most anticipated. And she viewed these sonnets, I think, as *performances*. Shakespeare's example, of course, towered over her desk, and she looked up to his tone and turns. Beyond that, she was aware of the sonnet's long tradition, and sought for her own a "classic" or timeless language, at once elevated and intimate. Other poets of the time forged their own idioms—albeit, in the case of a Wallace Stevens or a Hart Crane, they did so in more original ways. Millay wrote as one who wished to extend a tradition rather than upend it. She preferred to use a familiar language to speak of unfamiliar matters, the better to deal ironically with the heart's history. This is true, of course, of all her poems. They will strike many contemporary ears as overly literary, but that is just a scrim her colored lights are trained on. Stared through, that scrim yields to the stage set beyond, on which is played out the poem's emotional script.

Even in college, Millay knew she had a power to attract, and she used it to advance her prospects. "People fall in love with me," she wrote, "and annoy me and distress me and flatter me and excite me." And she responded in kind; there were torrid affairs with girls at school, adding to her campus notoriety, and tepid flings with older men who might help her career. Throughout her life, she did what she felt she must do in order to create the conditions necessary to accomplish her work. After Vassar, she became the Circe of Greenwich Village. She was soon the talk of the town. She drank and partied and had affairs, and was thereby the envy of all, and to young women in particular she was the free spirit that American Babbittry had stifled. Her affairs were sometimes of the heart, and sometimes more practical. The writers she took as lovers (and invariably kept as friends afterward)—men like Floyd Dell, Edmund Wilson, John Peale Bishop, and Arthur Davison Ficke—were in a position, as it were, to both teach and help her. And she had always been a quick study. The poems she wrote then—wild, cool, elusive—intoxicated the Jazz Babies. She had found the pulse of the new generation:

> My candle burns at both ends;
>   It will not last the night;
> But ah, my foes, and oh, my friends—
>   It gives a lovely light!

Her anti-war play, *Aria da Capo*, for the Provincetown Players was a stunning, sold-out success, and was merely the prelude to a tumultuous decade. The Roaring '20s were a bright blur: her promiscuity with men and women, abortions, adoring crowds, reading tours, long stays abroad where she might be tramping through Albania or dining with Brancusi in Paris and sitting for Man Ray. The books appeared regularly, and in 1923 she became the first woman to win the Pulitzer Prize for poetry. Finally there came a point when, in the words of Edmund Wilson, "she was tired of breaking hearts and spreading havoc." It was in 1923 as well that she married Eugen Boissevain, a handsome Dutch importer twelve years her senior. In one sense, the marriage mended her childhood. Boissevain was both husband and parent to Millay, intent on providing her with the stability and quiet she needed to write. He saw her through reading tours and hospital stays. He worked the farm, kept the accounts, arranged their social life.

In time, his magnanimity was sorely tested. Millay was in constant need of stimulants to stir her imagination.

In 1928, during a stop in Chicago on a reading tour, she was introduced to a 22-year-old poet named George Dillon. He was all profile, weak-willed, shyly homosexual. Millay was smitten at once, and by the next afternoon had written him a sonnet that begins "This beast that rends me in the sight of all, / This love, this longing, this oblivious thing, / That has me under as the last leaves fall." The first thing she did after they became lovers was tell her husband. Dillon tried to slip away from Millay's intensity, and the distance he kept from her Millay filled up with the poems that became her best collection, *Fatal Interview*. (The title is from lines by Donne: "By our first strange and fatal interview, / By all desires which thereof did ensue.") The book was published in 1931 and within months had sold 50,000 copies. She had returned to her husband, but her fixation with Dillon smoldered, and again they set up a ménage, this time in Paris, until she wore Dillon out—or was done with him for her purposes. It was during that time they collaborated on a translation of Baudelaire's *Fleurs du mal* that earned the approbation of Paul Valéry. She had done what all good writers do—behaved badly. Her ruthlessness had more charm than that of others, but Millay spared no one—least of all herself—in her drive to create the "havoc" her poems feed on, and then to surround herself with the solitude to work that chaos into shimmering lines.

Scandal, of course, only enhanced her celebrity. On Christmas Day 1932, she inaugurated her own series of nationwide radio broadcasts, reading her poems. For women, she made complicated passion real; for men, she made it alluring. The triumphal chariot rolled on, though the road was getting rockier. Reviews of her work were growing more mixed. Her critics resented her popularity, but in truth her work—except for flashes of lightning—

was dimming. Fate itself seemed to be greasing the slippery slope. While vacationing with her husband in Florida to finish a new book, *Conversation at Midnight*, their hotel burned down, her manuscript in the ashes. In 1936, a freakish car accident left her in severe pain, which in turn led to a dependence on drugs she never was able to overcome. Her final years are a sad parable of helplessness. Puffy and dumpy and slow, she must have looked like Eurydice back from the underworld. When Boissevain died suddenly in 1949, Millay merely went through the motions of life. A year later, alone at Steepletop, she sat at the top of the staircase, a bottle of wine beside her. At some point, she pitched forward, down the stairs, breaking her neck. She was 58. In her notebook, it was discovered that she had penciled a ring around the last three lines of a new poem she had drafted:

> I will control myself, or go inside.
> I will not flaw perfection with my grief,
> Handsome, this day: no matter who has died.

■

A word now about this book. It is the largest and most varied selection of Millay's work ever made, and several principles have helped determine the contents. First, all of her books have been represented, in order to give the reader a sense of the scope of her entire career. There are excerpts, for instance, from *Conversation at Midnight*. (After the manuscript was destroyed, she reconstructed it from memory.) This 1937 book-length sequence alternates poems in the voices of six men over after-dinner drinks. One is a wealthy bachelor, the others a priest, a Communist, a portrait painter, a stockbroker, and a writer. Their exchanges turn over the topics of modern life—politics, war, heroism, music, philosophy, and love. It is the sort of poem-as-symposium that, a decade later with *The Age of Anxiety*, Auden would perfect by charging it with a more focused set of themes and a keener verse technique. Still, reviewers at the time were intrigued by Millay's effort. The front page of *The New York Times Book Review*, for instance, called it "worldly, mature, objective, and dramatic ... it has brought a privateness of feeling into a world of thought ... it takes its place, in its own way, with Pound's *Cantos*, Eliot's *The Waste Land*, Crane's *The Bridge*, Auden's *The Orators*." Hindsight would dispute the comparisons, but there is no doubting Millay's interest in challenging her own facility or experimenting with form and voice. There is an excerpt here too from her 1942 *The Murder of Lidice*, occasioned by the massacre in a Czech village by Nazi troops. The Writers' War Board asked Millay to commemorate the event, and her poem, in an elaborate NBC broadcast narrated by Paul Muni, was heard all across the nation and beamed by shortwave to millions in Europe.

Second, I have tried to give the effect of several of her extended sequences by including them here in their entirety. All 52 sonnets of *Fatal Interview*—an almanac of love's seasons—are included, as well as all of "Epitaph for the Race of Man" and of her remarkable "Sonnets from an Ungrafted Tree," a dark, elliptical back-country narrative that rivals Frost.

Third, though I have included a few poems like "The Ballad of the Harp-Weaver" which I feel are inferior but recognize as milestones in her career, I have for the most part been guided by my taste for Millay at her tautest and truest. It should be remembered that she liked to sit down at the piano and play Mozart or Brahms; the best of her poems have the delicate complexities of a score, harmonic progressions and crucial motifs. There are precise and resonant images everywhere; they may animate a line and shape an entire poem, as they do "Ebb":

> I know what my heart is like
>   Since your love died:
> It is like a hollow ledge
> Holding a little pool
>   Left there by the tide,
>   A little tepid pool,
> Drying inward from the edge.

There is too an often overlooked epigrammatic quality to her poems. The fable in "The True Encounter," for example, is at once pithy and enigmatic:

> "Wolf!" cried my cunning heart
>   At every sheep it spied,
>   And roused the countryside.
>
> "Wolf! Wolf!"—and up would start
>   Good neighbours, bringing spade
>   And pitchfork to my aid.
>
> At length my cry was known:
>   Therein lay my release.
> I met the wolf alone
>   And was devoured in peace.

This quality sometimes rises to an eerie pitch. Take the early poem "Passer Mortuus Est" (the allusion is to Catullus's famous poem that begins *Luctus de morte passeris*, about his Lesbia's dead pet sparrow). I quote here its first two stanzas. The first is sharpened by its image of the narrow bed. The second ends by sounding like Emily Dickinson, unexpected and convincing:

Death devours all lovely things:
  Lesbia with her sparrow
Shares the darkness,—presently
  Every bed is narrow.

Unremembered as old rain
  Dries the sheer libation;
And the little petulant hand
  Is an annotation.

Fourth, I have included a section of verse rarities: her one-act play *Aria da Capo*, a section of her Baudelaire translations, and two excerpts from her libretto for Deems Taylor's opera *The King's Henchman*. The latter has disappeared from the repertoire, but at its premiere in 1927 at the Metropolitan Opera it was received rapturously. The starry cast came out for seventeen curtain calls. The opera went on a thirty-city tour. *The New Yorker* declared, "It is almost incontestable that the lyric drama of Miss Millay and Mr. Taylor is the greatest American opera so far." The libretto, a version of the Tristan and Isolde story but with a fascinating twist at the end that makes the heroine unsympathetic, is set in Anglo-Saxon times and uses no word (so the poet claimed) not then in use. There are passages of surpassing beauty, and two are included here—the heroine Ælfrida's conjuring song and the love duet between Ælfrida and her lover Æthelwold, set in passion's moonlit forest.

■

Of all the critical barbs aimed at Millay's poems over the years, few have not had real targets. Still, two dozen of her poems can stand among the best lyrics of the twentieth century, and all of her work urges re-discovery. In a sense, it was her misfortune to write at a time when the tide had turned in favor of the modernists, who felt as T. S. Eliot did when he wrote that "no artist produces great art by a deliberate attempt to express his own personality." Millay wrote from the bedroom, not the library. Eliot and Pound were expansionists, broadly addressing themselves to culture and ideas. Millay, on the other hand, wrote of the private life, of domestic scenes. The modernist poets preferred the anonymous collage, the reverberant fragment. Millay preferred the single voice, hushed or hieratic, but always the embodiment of the lyric impulse. After her death, fashions again changed. The confessional poets flayed the lyric to reveal garish details Millay's decorum would instinctively have avoided. And all along, though she was never forgotten by poets (Sylvia Plath and Anne Sexton studied her with admiration), critics eager to extol the skewed obliquities of the modernists or the "authenticity" of plain-speaking nativists ignored Millay. (Other poets shared her exile, of course. *Minor* was a convenient label to paste on those whose ambitions were different. Neither A. E. Housman nor Robert Graves could be found on the critical map. Elinor Wylie and Louise Bogan were "lady poets.") The neglect has kept us from a poet of genuine strength. Millay's emotional range may seem narrow, and her technique often limited to exquisite feelings dipped in a bitter irony. If the two strings on her lyre, love and death, both in the end sound the same note, still they ring variations on those dynamics of longing and loss that have inspired poets from Catullus to the Cavaliers, from Shelley to Cavafy and Lorca. And often because of these self-imposed restraints, Millay could write poems with an obsessed, haunting power—her best sonnets especially, each a silver cage for the melancholy, wingèd god of love—poems that expose the banalities of more burly or experimental styles, and continue to touch the heart, disturb the intelligence, and lodge in the memory.

J. D. McClatchy
2002

I

Renascence

All I could see from where I stood
Was three long mountains and a wood;
I turned and looked another way,
And saw three islands in a bay.
So with my eyes I traced the line
Of the horizon, thin and fine,
Straight around till I was come
Back to where I'd started from;
And all I saw from where I stood
Was three long mountains and a wood.

Over these things I could not see:
These were the things that bounded me.
And I could touch them with my hand,
Almost, I thought, from where I stand!
And all at once things seemed so small
My breath came short, and scarce at all.
But, sure, the sky is big, I said:
Miles and miles above my head.
So here upon my back I'll lie
And look my fill into the sky.
And so I looked, and after all,
The sky was not so very tall.
The sky, I said, must somewhere stop . . .

And—sure enough!—I see the top!
The sky, I thought, is not so grand;
I 'most could touch it with my hand!
And reaching up my hand to try,
I screamed, to feel it touch the sky.

I screamed, and—lo!—Infinity
Came down and settled over me;
Forced back my scream into my chest;
Bent back my arm upon my breast;
And, pressing of the Undefined
The definition on my mind,
Held up before my eyes a glass
Through which my shrinking sight did pass
Until it seemed I must behold
Immensity made manifold;
Whispered to me a word whose sound
Deafened the air for worlds around,
And brought unmuffled to my ears
The gossiping of friendly spheres,
The creaking of the tented sky,
The ticking of Eternity.

I saw and heard, and knew at last
The How and Why of all things, past,
And present, and forevermore.
The Universe, cleft to the core,
Lay open to my probing sense,
That, sickening, I would fain pluck thence
But could not,—nay! but needs must suck
At the great wound, and could not pluck

My lips away till I had drawn
All venom out.—Ah, fearful pawn:
For my omniscience paid I toll
In infinite remorse of soul.
All sin was of my sinning, all
Atoning mine, and mine the gall
Of all regret. Mine was the weight
Of every brooded wrong, the hate
That stood behind each envious thrust,
Mine every greed, mine every lust.

And all the while, for every grief,
Each suffering, I craved relief
With individual desire;
Craved all in vain! And felt fierce fire
About a thousand people crawl;
Perished with each,—then mourned for all!

A man was starving in Capri;
He moved his eyes and looked at me;
I felt his gaze, I heard his moan,
And knew his hunger as my own.

I saw at sea a great fog bank
Between two ships that struck and sank;
A thousand screams the heavens smote;
And every scream tore through my throat.

No hurt I did not feel, no death
That was not mine; mine each last breath
That, crying, met an answering cry

From the compassion that was I.
All suffering mine, and mine its rod;
Mine, pity like the pity of God.

Ah, awful weight! Infinity
Pressed down upon the finite Me!
My anguished spirit, like a bird,
Beating against my lips I heard;
Yet lay the weight so close about
There was no room for it without.
And so beneath the weight lay I
And suffered death, but could not die.

Long had I lain thus, craving death,
When quietly the earth beneath
Gave way, and inch by inch, so great
At last had grown the crushing weight,
Into the earth I sank till I
Full six feet under ground did lie,
And sank no more,—there is no weight
Can follow here, however great.
From off my breast I felt it roll,
And as it went my tortured soul
Burst forth and fled in such a gust
That all about me swirled the dust.

Deep in the earth I rested now.
Cool is its hand upon the brow
And soft its breast beneath the head
Of one who is so gladly dead.
And all at once, and over all
The pitying rain began to fall;

I lay and heard each pattering hoof
Upon my lowly, thatchèd roof,
And seemed to love the sound far more
Than ever I had done before.
For rain it hath a friendly sound
To one who's six feet under ground;
And scarce the friendly voice or face,
A grave is such a quiet place.

The rain, I said, is kind to come
And speak to me in my new home.
I would I were alive again
To kiss the fingers of the rain,
To drink into my eyes the shine
Of every slanting silver line,
To catch the freshened, fragrant breeze
From drenched and dripping apple-trees.
For soon the shower will be done,
And then the broad face of the sun
Will laugh above the rain-soaked earth
Until the world with answering mirth
Shakes joyously, and each round drop
Rolls, twinkling, from its grass-blade top.

How can I bear it, buried here,
While overhead the sky grows clear
And blue again after the storm?
O, multi-coloured, multi-form,
Belovèd beauty over me,
That I shall never, never see
Again! Spring-silver, autumn-gold,
That I shall never more behold!—

Sleeping your myriad magics through,
Close-sepulchred away from you!
O God, I cried, give me new birth,
And put me back upon the earth!
Upset each cloud's gigantic gourd
And let the heavy rain, down-poured
In one big torrent, set me free,
Washing my grave away from me!

I ceased; and through the breathless hush
That answered me, the far-off rush
Of herald wings came whispering
Like music down the vibrant string
Of my ascending prayer, and—crash!
Before the wild wind's whistling lash
The startled storm-clouds reared on high
And plunged in terror down the sky!
And the big rain in one black wave
Fell from the sky and struck my grave.

I know not how such things can be;
I only know there came to me
A fragrance such as never clings
To aught save happy living things;
A sound as of some joyous elf
Singing sweet songs to please himself,
And, through and over everything,
A sense of glad awakening.
The grass, a-tiptoe at my ear,
Whispering to me I could hear;
I felt the rain's cool finger-tips

Brushed tenderly across my lips,
Laid gently on my sealèd sight,
And all at once the heavy night
Fell from my eyes and I could see!—
A drenched and dripping apple-tree,
A last long line of silver rain,
A sky grown clear and blue again.
And as I looked a quickening gust
Of wind blew up to me and thrust
Into my face a miracle
Of orchard-breath, and with the smell,—
I know not how such things can be!—
I breathed my soul back into me.

Ah! Up then from the ground sprang I
And hailed the earth with such a cry
As is not heard save from a man
Who has been dead, and lives again.
About the trees my arms I wound;
Like one gone mad I hugged the ground;
I raised my quivering arms on high;
I laughed and laughed into the sky;
Till at my throat a strangling sob
Caught fiercely, and a great heart-throb
Sent instant tears into my eyes:
O God, I cried, no dark disguise
Can e'er hereafter hide from me
Thy radiant identity!
Thou canst not move across the grass
But my quick eyes will see Thee pass,
Nor speak, however silently,

But my hushed voice will answer Thee.
I know the path that tells Thy way
Through the cool eve of every day;
God, I can push the grass apart
And lay my finger on Thy heart!

The world stands out on either side
No wider than the heart is wide;
Above the world is stretched the sky,—
No higher than the soul is high.
The heart can push the sea and land
Farther away on either hand;
The soul can split the sky in two,
And let the face of God shine through.
But East and West will pinch the heart
That can not keep them pushed apart;
And he whose soul is flat—the sky
Will cave in on him by and by.

Interim

The room is full of you!—As I came in
And closed the door behind me, all at once
A something in the air, intangible,
Yet stiff with meaning, struck my senses sick!—

Sharp, unfamiliar odours have destroyed
Each other room's dear personality.
The heavy scent of damp, funeral flowers,—
The very essence, hush-distilled, of Death—

Has strangled that habitual breath of home
Whose expiration leaves all houses dead;
And wheresoe'er I look is hideous change.
Save here. Here 'twas as if a weed-choked gate
Had opened at my touch, and I had stepped
Into some long-forgot, enchanted, strange,
Sweet garden of a thousand years ago
And suddenly thought, "I have been here before!"

You are not here. I know that you are gone,
And will not ever enter here again.
And yet it seems to me, if I should speak,
Your silent step must wake across the hall;
If I should turn my head, that your sweet eyes
Would kiss me from the door.—So short a time
To teach my life its transposition to
This difficult and unaccustomed key!—

The room is as you left it; your last touch—
A thoughtless pressure, knowing not itself
As saintly—hallows now each simple thing;
Hallows and glorifies, and glows between
The dust's grey fingers like a shielded light.

There is your book, just as you laid it down,
Face to the table,—I cannot believe
That you are gone!—Just then it seemed to me
You must be here. I almost laughed to think
How like reality the dream had been;
Yet knew before I laughed, and so was still.
That book, outspread, just as you laid it down!

Perhaps you thought, "I wonder what comes next,
And whether this or this will be the end";
So rose, and left it, thinking to return.

Perhaps that chair, when you arose and passed
Out of the room, rocked silently a while
Ere it again was still. When you were gone
Forever from the room, perhaps that chair,
Stirred by your movement, rocked a little while,
Silently, to and fro . . .

And here are the last words your fingers wrote,
Scrawled in broad characters across a page
In this brown book I gave you. Here your hand,
Guiding your rapid pen, moved up and down.
Here with a looping knot you crossed a "t,"
And here another like it, just beyond
These two eccentric "e's." You were so small,
And wrote so brave a hand!

                        How strange it seems
That of all words these are the words you chose!
And yet a simple choice; you did not know
You would not write again. If you had known—
But then, it does not matter,—and indeed
If you had known there was so little time
You would have dropped your pen and come to me
And this page would be empty, and some phrase
Other than this would hold my wonder now.
Yet, since you could not know, and it befell
That these are the last words your fingers wrote,
There is a dignity some might not see

In this, "I picked the first sweet-pea today."
Today! Was there an opening bud beside it
You left until tomorrow?—O my love,
The things that withered,—and you came not back!
That day you filled this circle of my arms
That now is empty. (O my empty life!)
That day—that day you picked the first sweet-pea,—
And brought it in to show me! I recall
With terrible distinctness how the smell
Of your cool gardens drifted in with you.
I know, you held it up for me to see
And flushed because I looked not at the flower,
But at your face; and when behind my look
You saw such unmistakable intent
You laughed and brushed your flower against my lips.
(You were the fairest thing God ever made,
I think.) And then your hands above my heart
Drew down its stem into a fastening,
And while your head was bent I kissed your hair.
I wonder if you knew. (Belovèd hands!
Somehow I cannot seem to see them still.
Somehow I cannot seem to see the dust
In your bright hair.) What is the need of Heaven
When earth can be so sweet?—If only God
Had let us love,—and show the world the way!
Strange cancellings must ink the eternal books
When love-crossed-out will bring the answer right!

That first sweet-pea! I wonder where it is.
It seems to me I laid it down somewhere,
And yet,—I am not sure. I am not sure,

Even, if it was white or pink; for then
'Twas much like any other flower to me,
Save that it was the first. I did not know,
Then, that it was the last. If I had known—
But then, it does not matter. Strange how few,
After all's said and done, the things that are
Of moment.

        Few indeed! When I can make
Of ten small words a rope to hang the world!
"I had you and I have you now no more."
There, there it dangles,—where's the little truth
That can for long keep footing under that
When its slack syllables tighten to a thought?
Here, let me write it down! I wish to see
Just how a thing like that will look on paper!

   "I had you and I have you now no more."

O little words, how can you run so straight
Across the page, beneath the weight you bear?
How can you fall apart, whom such a theme
Has bound together, and hereafter aid
In trivial expression, that have been
So hideously dignified?

             Would God
That tearing you apart would tear the thread
I strung you on! Would God—O God, my mind
Stretches asunder on this merciless rack
Of imagery! Oh, let me sleep a while!
Would I could sleep, and wake to find me back
In that sweet summer afternoon with you.

Summer? 'Tis summer still by the calendar!
How easily could God, if He so willed,
Set back the world a little turn or two!—
Correct its griefs, and brings its joys again!

We were so wholly one I had not thought
That we could die apart. I had not thought
That I could move,—and you be stiff and still!
That I could speak,—and you perforce be dumb!
I think our heart-strings were, like warp and woof
In some firm fabric, woven in and out;
Your golden filaments in fair design
Across my duller fibre. And today
The shining strip is rent; the exquisite
Fine pattern is destroyed; part of your heart
Aches in my breast; part of my heart lies chilled
In the damp earth with you. I have been torn
In two, and suffer for the rest of me.
What is my life to me? And what am I
To life,—a ship whose star has guttered out?
A Fear that in the deep night starts awake
Perpetually, to find its senses strained
Against the taut strings of the quivering air,
Awaiting the return of some dread chord?

Dark, Dark, is all I find for metaphor;
All else were contrast;—save that contrast's wall
Is down, and all opposed things flow together
Into a vast monotony, where night
And day, and frost and thaw, and death and life,
Are synonyms. What now—what now to me

Are all the jabbering birds and foolish flowers
That clutter up the world? You were my song!
Now, now, let discord scream! You were my flower!
Now let the world grow weeds! For I shall not
Plant things above your grave—(the common balm
Of the conventional woe for its own wound!)
Amid sensations rendered negative
By your elimination stands today,
Certain, unmixed, the element of grief;
I sorrow; and I shall not mock my truth
With travesties of suffering, nor seek
To effigy its incorporeal bulk
In little wry-faced images of woe.
I cannot call you back; and I desire
No utterance of my immaterial voice.
I cannot even turn my face this way
Or that, and say, "My face is turned to you";
I know not where you are, I do not know
If heaven hold you or if earth transmute,
Body and soul, you into earth again;
But this I know:—not for one second's space
Shall I insult my sight with visionings
Such as the credulous crowd so eager-eyed
Beholds, self-conjured in the empty air.
Let the world wail! Let drip its easy tears!
My sorrow shall be dumb!

                    —What do I say?
God! God!—God pity me! Am I gone mad
That I should spit upon a rosary?
Am I become so shrunken? Would to God

I too might feel that frenzied faith whose touch
Makes temporal the most enduring grief;
Though it must walk a while, as is its wont,
With wild lamenting! Would I too might weep
Where weeps the world and hangs its piteous wreaths
For its new dead! Not Truth, but Faith, it is
That keeps the world alive. If all at once
Faith were to slacken,—that unconscious faith
Which must, I know, yet be the corner-stone
Of all believing,—birds now flying fearless
Across, would drop in terror to the earth;
Fishes would drown; and the all-governing reins
Would tangle in the frantic hands of God
And the worlds gallop headlong to destruction!

O God, I see it now, and my sick brain
Staggers and swoons! How often over me
Flashes this breathlessness of sudden sight
In which I see the universe unrolled
Before me like a scroll and read thereon
Chaos and Doom, where helpless planets whirl
Dizzily round and round and round and round,
Like tops across a table, gathering speed
With every spin, to waver on the edge
One instant—looking over—and the next
To shudder and lurch forward out of sight!

Ah, I am worn out—I am wearied out—
It is too much—I am but flesh and blood,
And I must sleep. Though you were dead again,
I am but flesh and blood and I must sleep.

Afternoon on a Hill

I will be the gladdest thing
    Under the sun!
I will touch a hundred flowers
    And not pick one.

I will look at cliffs and clouds
    With quiet eyes,
Watch the wind bow down the grass,
    And the grass rise.

And when lights begin to show
    Up from the town,
I will mark which must be mine,
    And then start down!

Witch-Wife

She is neither pink nor pale,
    And she never will be all mine;
She learned her hands in a fairy-tale,
    And her mouth on a valentine.

She has more hair than she needs;
    In the sun 'tis a woe to me!
And her voice is a string of coloured beads,
    Or steps leading into the sea.

She loves me all that she can,
    And her ways to my ways resign;
But she was not made for any man,
    And she never will be all mine.

When the Year Grows Old

I cannot but remember
    When the year grows old—
October—November—
    How she disliked the cold!

She used to watch the swallows
    Go down across the sky,
And turn from the window
    With a little sharp sigh.

And often when the brown leaves
    Were brittle on the ground,
And the wind in the chimney
    Made a melancholy sound,

She had a look about her
    That I wish I could forget—
The look of a scared thing
    Sitting in a net!

Oh, beautiful at nightfall
    The soft spitting snow!

And beautiful the bare boughs
　　Rubbing to and fro!

But the roaring of the fire,
　　And the warmth of fur,
And the boiling of the kettle
　　Were beautiful to her!

I cannot but remember
　　When the year grows old—
October—November—
　　How she disliked the cold!

———

Time does not bring relief; you all have lied
Who told me time would ease me of my pain!
I miss him in the weeping of the rain;
I want him at the shrinking of the tide;
The old snows melt from every mountain-side,
And last year's leaves are smoke in every lane;
But last year's bitter loving must remain
Heaped on my heart, and my old thoughts abide.
There are a hundred places where I fear
To go,—so with his memory they brim.
And entering with relief some quiet place
Where never fell his foot or shone his face
I say, "There is no memory of him here!"
And so stand stricken, so remembering him.

If I should learn, in some quite casual way,
That you were gone, not to return again—
Read from the back-page of a paper, say,
Held by a neighbor in a subway train,
How at the corner of this avenue
And such a street (so are the papers filled)
A hurrying man, who happened to be you,
At noon today had happened to be killed—
I should not cry aloud—I could not cry
Aloud, or wring my hands in such a place—
I should but watch the station lights rush by
With a more careful interest on my face;
Or raise my eyes and read with greater care
Where to store furs and how to treat the hair.

Bluebeard

This door you might not open, and you did;
So enter now, and see for what slight thing
You are betrayed. . . . Here is no treasure hid,
No cauldron, no clear crystal mirroring
The sought-for Truth, no heads of women slain
For greed like yours, no writhings of distress;
But only what you see. . . . Look yet again:
An empty room, cobwebbed and comfortless.
Yet this alone out of my life I kept
Unto myself, lest any know me quite;
And you did so profane me when you crept
Unto the threshold of this room tonight
That I must never more behold your face.
This now is yours. I seek another place.

First Fig

My candle burns at both ends;
   It will not last the night;
But ah, my foes, and oh, my friends—
   It gives a lovely light!

Second Fig

Safe upon the solid rock the ugly houses stand:
Come and see my shining palace built upon the sand!

Recuerdo

We were very tired, we were very merry—
We had gone back and forth all night on the ferry.
It was bare and bright, and smelled like a stable—
But we looked into a fire, we leaned across a table,
We lay on a hill-top underneath the moon;
And the whistles kept blowing, and the dawn came soon.

We were very tired, we were very merry—
We had gone back and forth all night on the ferry;
And you ate an apple, and I ate a pear,

From a dozen of each we had bought somewhere;
And the sky went wan, and the wind came cold,
And the sun rose dripping, a bucketful of gold.

We were very tired, we were very merry,
We had gone back and forth all night on the ferry.
We hailed, "Good morrow, mother!" to a shawl-covered
        head,
And bought a morning paper, which neither of us read;
And she wept, "God bless you!" for the apples and pears,
And we gave her all our money but our subway fares.

To the Not Impossible Him

How shall I know, unless I go
    To Cairo and Cathay,
Whether or not this blessèd spot
    Is blest in every way?

Now it may be, the flower for me
    Is this beneath my nose;
How shall I tell, unless I smell
    The Carthaginian rose?

The fabric of my faithful love
    No power shall dim or ravel
Whilst I stay here,—but oh, my dear,
    If I should ever travel!

Grown-up

Was it for this I uttered prayers,
And sobbed and cursed and kicked the stairs,
That now, domestic as a plate,
I should retire at half-past eight?

Daphne

Why do you follow me?—
Any moment I can be
Nothing but a laurel-tree.

Any moment of the chase
I can leave you in my place
A pink bough for your embrace.

Yet if over hill and hollow
Still it is your will to follow,
I am off;—to heel, Apollo!

Midnight Oil

Cut if you will, with Sleep's dull knife,
    Each day to half its length, my friend,—
The years that Time takes off *my* life,
    He'll take from off the other end!

The Philosopher

And what are you that, wanting you,
   I should be kept awake
As many nights as there are days
   With weeping for your sake?

And what are you that, missing you,
   As many days as crawl
I should be listening to the wind
   And looking at the wall?

I know a man that's a braver man
   And twenty men as kind,
And what are you, that you should be
   The one man in my mind?

Yet women's ways are witless ways,
   As any sage will tell,—
And what am I, that I should love
   So wisely and so well?

———

I think I should have loved you presently,
And given in earnest words I flung in jest;
And lifted honest eyes for you to see,
And caught your hand against my cheek and breast;

And all my pretty follies flung aside
That won you to me, and beneath your gaze,
Naked of reticence and shorn of pride,
Spread like a chart my little wicked ways.
I, that had been to you, had you remained,
But one more waking from a recurrent dream,
Cherish no less the certain stakes I gained,
And walk your memory's halls, austere, supreme,
A ghost in marble of a girl you knew
Who would have loved you in a day or two.

———

I shall forget you presently, my dear,
So make the most of this, your little day,
Your little month, your little half a year,
Ere I forget, or die, or move away,
And we are done forever; by and by
I shall forget you, as I said, but now,
If you entreat me with your loveliest lie
I will protest you with my favourite vow.
I would indeed that love were longer-lived,
And oaths were not so brittle as they are,
But so it is, and nature has contrived
To struggle on without a break thus far,—
Whether or not we find what we are seeking
Is idle, biologically speaking.

Eel-Grass

No matter what I say,
   All that I really love
Is the rain that flattens on the bay,
   And the eel-grass in the cove;
The jingle-shells that lie and bleach
   At the tide-line, and the trace
Of higher tides along the beach:
   Nothing in this place.

Elegy Before Death

There will be rose and rhododendron
   When you are dead and under ground;
Still will be heard from white syringas
   Heavy with bees, a sunny sound;

Still will the tamaracks be raining
   After the rain has ceased, and still
Will there be robins in the stubble,
   Grey sheep upon the warm green hill.

Spring will not ail nor autumn falter;
   Nothing will know that you are gone,—
Saving alone some sullen plough-land
   None but yourself sets foot upon;

Saving the may-weed and the pig-weed
  Nothing will know that you are dead,—
These, and perhaps a useless wagon
  Standing beside some tumbled shed.

Oh, there will pass with your great passing
  Little of beauty not your own,—
Only the light from common water,
  Only the grace from simple stone!

Weeds

White with daisies and red with sorrel
  And empty, empty under the sky!—
Life is a quest and love a quarrel—
  Here is a place for me to lie.

Daisies spring from damnèd seeds,
  And this red fire that here I see
Is a worthless crop of crimson weeds,
  Cursed by farmers thriftily.

But here, unhated for an hour,
  The sorrel runs in ragged flame,
The daisy stands, a bastard flower,
  Like flowers that bear an honest name.

And here a while, where no wind brings
  The baying of a pack athirst,
May sleep the sleep of blessèd things,
  The blood too bright, the brow accurst.

Passer Mortuus Est

Death devours all lovely things:
   Lesbia with her sparrow
Shares the darkness,—presently
   Every bed is narrow.

Unremembered as old rain
   Dries the sheer libation;
And the little petulant hand
   Is an annotation.

After all, my erstwhile dear,
   My no longer cherished,
Need we say it was not love,
   Just because it perished?

Alms

My heart is what it was before,
   A house where people come and go;
But it is winter with your love,
   The sashes are beset with snow.

I light the lamp and lay the cloth,
   I blow the coals to blaze again;
But it is winter with your love,
   The frost is thick upon the pane.

I know a winter when it comes:
   The leaves are listless on the boughs;

I watched your love a little while,
  And brought my plants into the house.

I water them and turn them south,
  I snap the dead brown from the stem;
But it is winter with your love,
  I only tend and water them.

There was a time I stood and watched
  The small, ill-natured sparrows' fray;
I loved the beggar that I fed,
  I cared for what he had to say,

I stood and watched him out of sight;
  Today I reach around the door
And set a bowl upon the step;
  My heart is what it was before,

But it is winter with your love;
  I scatter crumbs upon the sill,
And close the window,—and the birds
  May take or leave them, as they will.

Inland

People that build their houses inland,
  People that buy a plot of ground
Shaped like a house, and build a house there,
  Far from the sea-board, far from the sound

Of water sucking the hollow ledges,
    Tons of water striking the shore,—
What do they long for, as I long for
    One salt smell of the sea once more?

People the waves have not awakened,
    Spanking the boats at the harbour's head,
What do they long for, as I long for,—
    Starting up in my inland bed,

Beating the narrow walls, and finding
    Neither a window nor a door,
Screaming to God for death by drowning,—
    One salt taste of the sea once more?

Ebb

I know what my heart is like
    Since your love died:
It is like a hollow ledge
Holding a little pool
    Left there by the tide,
    A little tepid pool,
Drying inward from the edge.

FROM **Memorial to D. C.**

(Vassar College, 1918)

I. *Epitaph*

Heap not on this mound
  Roses that she loved so well;
Why bewilder her with roses,
  That she cannot see or smell?

She is happy where she lies
With the dust upon her eyes.

IV. *Dirge*

Boys and girls that held her dear,
  Do your weeping now;
All you loved of her lies here.

Brought to earth the arrogant brow,
  And the withering tongue
Chastened; do your weeping now.

Sing whatever songs are sung,
  Wind whatever wreath,
For a playmate perished young,
  For a spirit spent in death.

Boys and girls that held her dear,
All you loved of her lies here.

V. Elegy

Let them bury your big eyes
In the secret earth securely,
Your thin fingers, and your fair,
Soft, indefinite-coloured hair,—
All of these in some way, surely,
From the secret earth shall rise;
Not for these I sit and stare,
Broken and bereft completely:
Your young flesh that sat so neatly
On your little bones will sweetly
Blossom in the air.

But your voice . . . never the rushing
Of a river underground,
Not the rising of the wind
In the trees before the rain,
Not the woodcock's watery call,
Not the note the white-throat utters,
Not the feet of children pushing
Yellow leaves along the gutters
In the blue and bitter fall,
Shall content my musing mind
For the beauty of that sound
That in no new way at all
Ever will be heard again.

Sweetly through the sappy stalk
Of the vigourous weed,
Holding all it held before,
Cherished by the faithful sun,

On and on eternally
Shall your altered fluid run,
Bud and bloom and go to seed:
But your singing days are done;
But the music of your talk
Never shall the chemistry
Of the secret earth restore.
All your lovely words are spoken.
Once the ivory box is broken,
Beats the golden bird no more.

———

Only until this cigarette is ended,
A little moment at the end of all,
While on the floor the quiet ashes fall,
And in the firelight to a lance extended,
Bizarrely with the jazzing music blended,
The broken shadow dances on the wall,
I will permit my memory to recall
The vision of you, by all my dreams attended.
And then adieu,—farewell!—the dream is done.
Yours is a face of which I can forget
The colour and the features, every one,
The words not ever, and the smiles not yet;
But in your day this moment is the sun
Upon a hill, after the sun has set.

―――

Once more into my arid days like dew,
Like wind from an oasis, or the sound
Of cold sweet water bubbling underground,
A treacherous messenger, the thought of you
Comes to destroy me; once more I renew
Firm faith in your abundance, whom I found
Long since to be but just one other mound
Of sand, whereon no green thing ever grew.
And once again, and wiser in no wise,
I chase your coloured phantom on the air,
And sob and curse and fall and weep and rise
And stumble pitifully on to where,
Miserable and lost, with stinging eyes,
Once more I clasp,—and there is nothing there.

―――

When I too long have looked upon your face,
Wherein for me a brightness unobscured
Save by the mists of brightness has its place,
And terrible beauty not to be endured,
I turn away reluctant from your light,
And stand irresolute, a mind undone,
A silly, dazzled thing deprived of sight
From having looked too long upon the sun.

Then is my daily life a narrow room
In which a little while, uncertainly,
Surrounded by impenetrable gloom,
Among familiar things grown strange to me
Making my way, I pause, and feel, and hark,
Till I become accustomed to the dark.

———

And you as well must die, belovèd dust,
And all your beauty stand you in no stead;
This flawless, vital hand, this perfect head,
This body of flame and steel, before the gust
Of Death, or under his autumnal frost,
Shall be as any leaf, be no less dead
Than the first leaf that fell,—this wonder fled,
Altered, estranged, disintegrated, lost.
Nor shall my love avail you in your hour.
In spite of all my love, you will arise
Upon that day and wander down the air
Obscurely as the unattended flower,
It mattering not how beautiful you were,
Or how belovèd above all else that dies.

As to some lovely temple, tenantless
Long since, that once was sweet with shivering brass,
Knowing well its altars ruined and the grass
Grown up between the stones, yet from excess
Of grief hard driven, or great loneliness,
The worshiper returns, and those who pass
Marvel him crying on a name that was,—
So is it now with me in my distress.
Your body was a temple to Delight;
Cold are its ashes whence the breath is fled;
Yet here one time your spirit was wont to move;
Here might I hope to find you day or night;
And here I come to look for you, my love,
Even now, foolishly, knowing you are dead.

Wild Swans

I looked in my heart while the wild swans went over.
And what did I see I had not seen before?
Only a question less or a question more;
Nothing to match the flight of wild birds flying.
Tiresome heart, forever living and dying,
House without air, I leave you and lock your door.
Wild swans, come over the town, come over
The town again, trailing your legs and crying!

Autumn Chant

Now the autumn shudders
   In the rose's root.
Far and wide the ladders
   Lean among the fruit.

Now the autumn clambers
   Up the trellised frame,
And the rose remembers
   The dust from which it came.

Brighter than the blossom
   On the rose's bough
Sits the wizened, orange,
   Bitter berry now;

Beauty never slumbers;
   All is in her name;
But the rose remembers
   The dust from which it came.

Feast

I drank at every vine.
   The last was like the first.
I came upon no wine
   So wonderful as thirst.

I gnawed at every root.
   I ate of every plant.
I came upon no fruit
   So wonderful as want.

Feed the grape and bean
   To the vintner and monger;
I will lie down lean
   With my thirst and my hunger.

The Betrothal

Oh, come, my lad, or go, my lad,
And love me if you like.
I shall not hear the door shut
Nor the knocker strike.

Oh, bring me gifts or beg me gifts,
And wed me if you will.
I'd make a man a good wife,
Sensible and still.

And why should I be cold, my lad,
And why should you repine,

Because I love a dark head
That never will be mine?

I might as well be easing you
As lie alone in bed
And waste the night in wanting
A cruel dark head.

You might as well be calling yours
What never will be his,
And one of us be happy.
There's few enough as is.

The Ballad of the Harp-Weaver

"Son," said my mother,
    When I was knee-high,
"You've need of clothes to cover you,
    And not a rag have I.

"There's nothing in the house
    To make a boy breeches,
Nor shears to cut a cloth with,
    Nor thread to take stitches.

"There's nothing in the house
    But a loaf-end of rye,
And a harp with a woman's head
    Nobody will buy,"
    And she began to cry.

That was in the early fall.
　　When came the late fall,
"Son," she said, "the sight of you
　　Makes your mother's blood crawl,—

"Little skinny shoulder-blades
　　Sticking through your clothes!
And where you'll get a jacket from
　　God above knows.

"It's lucky for me, lad,
　　Your daddy's in the ground,
And can't see the way I let
　　His son go around!"
　　And she made a queer sound.

That was in the late fall.
　　When the winter came,
I'd not a pair of breeches
　　Nor a shirt to my name.

I couldn't go to school,
　　Or out of doors to play.
And all the other little boys
　　Passed our way.

"Son," said my mother,
　　"Come, climb into my lap,
And I'll chafe your little bones
　　While you take a nap."

And, oh, but we were silly
　　For half an hour or more,

Me with my long legs
    Dragging on the floor,

A-rock-rock-rocking
    To a mother-goose rhyme!
Oh, but we were happy
    For half an hour's time!

But there was I, a great boy,
    And what would folks say
To hear my mother singing me
    To sleep all day,
    In such a daft way?

Men say the winter
    Was bad that year;
Fuel was scarce,
    And food was dear.

A wind with a wolf's head
    Howled about our door,
And we burned up the chairs
    And sat upon the floor.

All that was left us
    Was a chair we couldn't break,
And the harp with a woman's head
    Nobody would take,
    For song or pity's sake.

The night before Christmas
    I cried with the cold,

I cried myself to sleep
    Like a two-year-old.

And in the deep night
    I felt my mother rise,
And stare down upon me
    With love in her eyes.

I saw my mother sitting
    On the one good chair,
A light falling on her
    From I couldn't tell where,

Looking nineteen,
    And not a day older,
And the harp with a woman's head
    Leaned against her shoulder.

Her thin fingers, moving
    In the thin, tall strings,
Were weav-weav-weaving
    Wonderful things.

Many bright threads,
    From where I couldn't see,
Were running through the harp-strings
    Rapidly,

And gold threads whistling
    Through my mother's hand.
I saw the web grow,
    And the pattern expand.

She wove a child's jacket,
    And when it was done
She laid it on the floor
    And wove another one.

She wove a red cloak
    So regal to see,
"She's made it for a king's son,"
    I said, "and not for me."
    But I knew it was for me.

She wove a pair of breeches
    Quicker than that!
She wove a pair of boots
    And a little cocked hat.

She wove a pair of mittens,
    She wove a little blouse,
She wove all night
    In the still, cold house.

She sang as she worked,
    And the harp-strings spoke;
Her voice never faltered,
    And the thread never broke.
    And when I awoke,—

There sat my mother
    With the harp against her shoulder,
Looking nineteen,
    And not a day older,

A smile about her lips,
    And a light about her head,
And her hands in the harp-strings
    Frozen dead.

And piled up beside her
    And toppling to the skies,
Were the clothes of a king's son,
    Just my size.

Never May the Fruit Be Plucked

Never, never may the fruit be plucked from the bough
And gathered into barrels.
He that would eat of love must eat it where it hangs.
Though the branches bend like reeds,
Though the ripe fruit splash in the grass or wrinkle
        on the tree,
He that would eat of love may bear away with him
Only what his belly can hold,
Nothing in the apron,
Nothing in the pockets.
Never, never may the fruit be gathered from the bough
And harvested in barrels.
The winter of love is a cellar of empty bins,
In an orchard soft with rot.

Hyacinth

I am in love with him to whom a hyacinth is dearer
Than I shall ever be dear.
On nights when the field-mice are abroad he cannot
    sleep:
He hears their narrow teeth at the bulbs of his hyacinths.
But the gnawing at my heart he does not hear.

To One Who Might Have Borne a Message

Had I known that you were going
I would have given you messages for her,
Now two years dead,
Whom I shall always love.

As it is, should she entreat you how it goes with me,
You must reply: as well as with most, you fancy;
That I love easily, and pass the time.

And she will not know how all day long between
My life and me her shadow intervenes,
A young thin girl,
Wearing a white skirt and a purple sweater
And a narrow pale blue ribbon about her hair.

I used to say to her, "I love you
Because your face is such a pretty colour,

No other reason."
But it was not true.

Oh, had I only known that you were going,
I could have given you messages for her!

———

Love is not blind. I see with single eye
Your ugliness and other women's grace.
I know the imperfection of your face,—
The eyes too wide apart, the brow too high
For beauty. Learned from earliest youth am I
In loveliness, and cannot so erase
Its letters from my mind, that I may trace
You faultless, I must love until I die.
More subtle is the sovereignty of love:
So am I caught that when I say, "Not fair,"
'Tis but as if I said, "Not here—not there—
Not risen—not writing letters." Well I know
What is this beauty men are babbling of;
I wonder only why they prize it so.

———

Pity me not because the light of day
At close of day no longer walks the sky;

Pity me not for beauties passed away
From field and thicket as the year goes by;
Pity me not the waning of the moon,
Nor that the ebbing tide goes out to sea,
Nor that a man's desire is hushed so soon,
And you no longer look with love on me.
This have I known always: Love is no more
Than the wide blossom which the wind assails,
Than the great tide that treads the shifting shore,
Strewing fresh wreckage gathered in the gales:
Pity me that the heart is slow to learn
What the swift mind beholds at every turn.

———

Here is a wound that never will heal, I know,
Being wrought not of a dearness and a death,
But of a love turned ashes and the breath
Gone out of beauty; never again will grow
The grass on that scarred acre, though I sow
Young seed there yearly and the sky bequeath
Its friendly weathers down, far underneath
Shall be such bitterness of an old woe.
That April should be shattered by a gust,
That August should be levelled by a rain,
I can endure, and that the lifted dust
Of man should settle to the earth again;
But that a dream can die, will be a thrust
Between my ribs forever of hot pain.

———

Your face is like a chamber where a king
Dies of his wounds, untended and alone,
Stifling with courteous gesture the crude moan
That speaks too loud of mortal perishing,
Rising on elbow in the dark to sing
Some rhyme now out of season but well known
In days when banners in his face were blown
And every woman had a rose to fling.
I know that through your eyes which look on me
Who stand regarding you with pitiful breath,
You see beyond the moment's pause, you see
The sunny sky, the skimming bird beneath,
And, fronting on your windows hopelessly.
Black in the noon, the broad estates of Death.

———

I, being born a woman and distressed
By all the needs and notions of my kind,
Am urged by your propinquity to find
Your person fair, and feel a certain zest
To bear your body's weight upon my breast:
So subtly is the fume of life designed,
To clarify the pulse and cloud the mind,
And leave me once again undone, possessed.
Think not for this, however, the poor treason
Of my stout blood against my staggering brain,

I shall remember you with love, or season
My scorn with pity,—let me make it plain:
I find this frenzy insufficient reason
For conversation when we meet again.

———

What lips my lips have kissed, and where, and why,
I have forgotten, and what arms have lain
Under my head till morning; but the rain
Is full of ghosts tonight, that tap and sigh
Upon the glass and listen for reply,
And in my heart there stirs a quiet pain
For unremembered lads that not again
Will turn to me at midnight with a cry.
Thus in the winter stands the lonely tree,
Nor knows what birds have vanished one by one,
Yet knows its boughs more silent than before:
I cannot say what loves have come and gone,
I only know that summer sang in me
A little while, that in me sings no more.

———

How healthily their feet upon the floor
Strike down! These are no spirits, but a band
Of children, surely, leaping hand in hand

Into the air in groups of three and four,
Wearing their silken rags as if they wore
Leaves only and light grasses, or a strand
Of black elusive seaweed oozing sand,
And running hard as if along a shore.
I know how lost forever, and at length
How still these lovely tossing limbs shall lie,
And the bright laughter and the panting breath;
And yet, before such beauty and such strength,
Once more, as always when the dance is high,
I am rebuked that I believe in death.

———

Euclid alone has looked on Beauty bare.
Let all who prate of Beauty hold their peace,
And lay them prone upon the earth and cease
To ponder on themselves, the while they stare
At nothing, intricately drawn nowhere
In shapes of shifting lineage; let geese
Gabble and hiss, but heroes seek release
From dusty bondage into luminous air.
O blinding hour, O holy, terrible day,
When first the shaft into his vision shone
Of light anatomized! Euclid alone
Has looked on Beauty bare. Fortunate they
Who, though once only and then but far away,
Have heard her massive sandal set on stone.

Sonnets from an Ungrafted Tree

I

So she came back into his house again
And watched beside his bed until he died,
Loving him not at all. The winter rain
Splashed in the painted butter-tub outside,
Where once her red geraniums had stood,
Where still their rotted stalks were to be seen;
The thin log snapped; and she went out for wood,
Bareheaded, running the few steps between
The house and shed; there, from the sodden eaves
Blown back and forth on ragged ends of twine,
Saw the dejected creeping-jinny vine
(And one, big-aproned, blithe, with stiff blue sleeves
Rolled to the shoulder that warm day in spring,
Who planted seeds, musing ahead to their far
    blossoming).

II

The last white sawdust on the floor was grown
Gray as the first, so long had he been ill;
The axe was nodding in the block; fresh-blown
And foreign came the rain across the sill,
But on the roof so steadily it drummed
She could not think a time it might not be—
In hazy summer, when the hot air hummed
With mowing, and locusts rising raspingly,
When that small bird with iridescent wings
And long incredible sudden silver tongue
Had just flashed (and yet maybe not!) among

The dwarf nasturtiums—when no sagging springs
Of shower were in the whole bright sky, somehow
Upon this roof the rain would drum as it was
     drumming now.

III

She filled her arms with wood, and set her chin
Forward, to hold the highest stick in place,
No less afraid than she had always been
Of spiders up her arms and on her face,
But too impatient for a careful search
Or a less heavy loading, from the heap
Selecting hastily small sticks of birch,
For their curled bark, that instantly will leap
Into a blaze, nor thinking to return
Some day, distracted, as of old, to find
Smooth, heavy, round, green logs with a wet, gray rind
Only, and knotty chunks that will not burn
(That day when dust is on the wood-box floor,
And some old catalogue, and a brown, shriveled
     apple core).

IV

The white bark writhed and sputtered like a fish
Upon the coals, exuding odorous smoke.
She knelt and blew, in a surging desolate wish
For comfort; and the sleeping ashes woke
And scattered to the hearth, but no thin fire
Broke suddenly, the wood was wet with rain.
Then, softly stepping forth from her desire,
(Being mindful of like passion hurled in vain

Upon a similar task, in other days)
She thrust her breath against the stubborn coal,
Bringing to bear upon its hilt the whole
Of her still body . . . there sprang a little blaze . . .
A pack of hounds, the flame swept up the flue!—
And the blue night stood flattened against the window,
     staring through.

v

A wagon stopped before the house; she heard
The heavy oilskins of the grocer's man
Slapping against his legs. Of a sudden whirred
Her heart like a frightened partridge, and she ran
And slid the bolt, leaving his entrance free;
Then in the cellar way till he was gone
Hid, breathless, praying that he might not see
The chair sway she had laid her hand upon
In passing. Sour and damp from that dark vault
Arose to her the well-remembered chill;
She saw the narrow wooden stairway still
Plunging into the earth, and the thin salt
Crusting the crocks; until she knew him far,
So stood, with listening eyes upon the empty
     doughnut jar.

vi

Then cautiously she pushed the cellar door
And stepped into the kitchen—saw the track
Of muddy rubber boots across the floor,
The many paper parcels in a stack
Upon the dresser; with accustomed care

Removed the twine and put the wrappings by,
Folded, and the bags flat, that with an air
Of ease had been whipped open skillfully,
To the gape of children. Treacherously dear
And simple was the dull, familiar task.
And so it was she came at length to ask:
How came the soda there? The sugar here?
Then the dream broke. Silent, she brought the mop,
And forced the trade-slip on the nail that held his
    razor strop.

VII

One way there was of muting in the mind
A little while the ever-clamorous care;
And there was rapture, of a decent kind,
In making mean and ugly objects fair:
Soft-sooted kettle-bottoms, that had been
Time after time set in above the fire,
Faucets, and candlesticks, corroded green,
To mine again from quarry; to attire
The shelves in paper petticoats, and tack
New oilcloth in the ringed-and-rotten's place,
Polish the stove till you could see your face,
And after nightfall rear an aching back
In a changed kitchen, bright as a new pin,
An advertisement, far too fine to cook a supper in.

VIII

She let them leave their jellies at the door
And go away, reluctant, down the walk.

She heard them talking as they passed before
The blind, but could not quite make out their talk
For noise in the room—the sudden heavy fall
And roll of a charred log, and the roused shower
Of snapping sparks; then sharply from the wall
The unforgivable crowing of the hour.
One instant set ajar, her quiet ear
Was stormed and forced by the full rout of day:
The rasp of a saw, the fussy cluck and bray
Of hens, the wheeze of a pump, she needs must hear;
She inescapably must endure to feel
Across her teeth the grinding of a backing wagon
    wheel.

IX

Not over-kind nor over-quick in study
Nor skilled in sports nor beautiful was he,
Who had come into her life when anybody
Would have been welcome, so in need was she.
They had become acquainted in this way:
He flashed a mirror in her eyes at school;
By which he was distinguished; from that day
They went about together, as a rule.
She told, in secret and with whispering,
How he had flashed a mirror in her eyes;
And as she told, it struck her with surprise
That this was not so wonderful a thing.
But what's the odds?—It's pretty nice to know
You've got a friend to keep you company everywhere
    you go.

X

She had forgotten how the August night
Was level as a lake beneath the moon,
In which she swam a little, losing sight
Of shore; and how the boy, who was at noon
Simple enough, not different from the rest,
Wore now a pleasant mystery as he went,
Which seemed to her an honest enough test
Whether she loved him, and she was content.
So loud, so loud the million crickets' choir . . .
So sweet the night, so long-drawn-out and late . . .
And if the man were not her spirit's mate,
Why was her body sluggish with desire?
Stark on the open field the moonlight fell,
But the oak tree's shadow was deep and black and secret
    as a well.

XI

It came into her mind, seeing how the snow
Was gone, and the brown grass exposed again,
And clothes-pins, and an apron—long ago,
In some white storm that sifted through the pane
And sent her forth reluctantly at last
To gather in, before the line gave way,
Garments, board-stiff, that galloped on the blast
Clashing like angel armies in a fray,
An apron long ago in such a night
Blown down and buried in the deepening drift,
To lie till April thawed it back to sight,
Forgotten, quaint and novel as a gift—

It struck her, as she pulled and pried and tore,
That here was spring, and the whole year to be lived
    through once more.

XII

Tenderly, in those times, as though she fed
An ailing child—with sturdy propping up
Of its small, feverish body in the bed,
And steadying of its hands about the cup—
She gave her husband of her body's strength,
Thinking of men, what helpless things they were,
Until he turned and fell asleep at length,
And stealthily stirred the night and spoke to her.
Familiar, at such moments, like a friend,
Whistled far off the long, mysterious train,
And she could see in her mind's vision plain
The magic World, where cities stood on end . . .
Remote from where she lay—and yet—between,
Save for something asleep beside her, only the window
    screen.

XIII

From the wan dream that was her waking day,
Wherein she journeyed, borne along the ground
Without her own volition in some way,
Or fleeing, motionless, with feet fast bound,
Or running silent through a silent house
Sharply remembered from an earlier dream,
Upstairs, down other stairs, fearful to rouse,
Regarding him, the wide and empty scream

Of a strange sleeper on a malignant bed,
And all the time not certain if it were
Herself so doing or some one like to her,
From this wan dream that was her daily bread,
Sometimes, at night, incredulous, she would wake—
A child, blowing bubbles that the chairs and carpet did
    not break!

    xiv

She had a horror he would die at night.
And sometimes when the light began to fade
She could not keep from noticing how white
The birches looked—and then she would be afraid,
Even with a lamp, to go about the house
And lock the windows; and as night wore on
Toward morning, if a dog howled, or a mouse
Squeaked in the floor, long after it was gone
Her flesh would sit awry on her. By day
She would forget somewhat, and it would seem
A silly thing to go with just this dream
And get a neighbor to come at night and stay.
But it would strike her sometimes, making the tea:
She had kept that kettle boiling all night long, for company.

    xv

There was upon the sill a pencil mark,
Vital with shadow when the sun stood still
At noon, but now, because the day was dark,
It was a pencil mark upon the sill.
And the mute clock, maintaining ever the same

Dead moment, blank and vacant of itself,
Was a pink shepherdess, a picture frame,
A shell marked Souvenir, there on the shelf.
Whence it occurred to her that he might be,
The mainspring being broken in his mind,
A clock himself, if one were so inclined,
That stood at twenty minutes after three—
The reason being for this, it might be said,
That things in death were neither clocks nor people,
    but only dead.

XVI

The doctor asked her what she wanted done
With him, that could not lie there many days.
And she was shocked to see how life goes on
Even after death, in irritating ways;
And mused how if he had not died at all
'Twould have been easier—then there need not be
The stiff disorder of a funeral
Everywhere, and the hideous industry,
And crowds of people calling her by name
And questioning her, she'd never seen before,
But only watching by his bed once more
And sitting silent if a knocking came . . .
She said at length, feeling the doctor's eyes,
"I don't know what you do exactly when a person dies."

XVII

Gazing upon him now, severe and dead,
It seemed a curious thing that she had lain

Beside him many a night in that cold bed,
And that had been which would not be again.
From his desirous body the great heat
Was gone at last, it seemed, and the taut nerves
Loosened forever. Formally the sheet
Set forth for her today those heavy curves
And lengths familiar as the bedroom door.
She was as one who enters, sly, and proud,
To where her husband speaks before a crowd,
And sees a man she never saw before—
The man who eats his victuals at her side,
Small, and absurd, and hers: for once, not hers,
        unclassified.

To the Wife of a Sick Friend

Shelter this candle from the wind.
Hold it steady. In its light
The cave wherein we wander lost
Glitters with frosty stalactite,
Blossoms with mineral rose and lotus,
Sparkles with crystal moon and star,
Till a man would rather be lost than found:
We have forgotten where we are.

Shelter this candle. Shrewdly blowing
Down the cave from a secret door
Enters our only foe, the wind.
Hold it steady. Lest we stand,
Each in a sudden, separate dark,
The hot wax spattered upon your hand,
The smoking wick in my nostrils strong,
The inner eyelid red and green
For a moment yet with moons and roses,—
Then the unmitigated dark.

Alone, alone, in a terrible place,
In utter dark without a face,
With only the dripping of the water on the stone,
And the sound of your tears, and the taste of my own.

To a Friend Estranged from Me

Now goes under, and I watch it go under, the sun
That will not rise again.
Today has seen the setting, in your eyes cold and
    senseless as the sea,
Of friendship better than bread, and of bright charity
That lifts a man a little above the beasts that run.

That this could be!
That I should live to see
Most vulgar Pride, that stale obstreperous clown,
So fitted out with purple robe and crown
To stand among his betters! Face to face
With outraged me in this once holy place,
Where Wisdom was a favoured guest and hunted Truth
    was harboured out of danger,
He bulks enthroned, a lewd, an insupportable stranger!

I would have sworn, indeed I swore it:
The hills may shift, the waters may decline,
Winter may twist the stem from the twig that bore it,
But never your love from me, your hand from mine.

Now goes under the sun, and I watch it go under.
Farewell, sweet light, great wonder!
You, too, farewell,—but fare not well enough to dream
You have done wisely to invite the night before the
    darkness came.

The Buck in the Snow

White sky, over the hemlocks bowed with snow,
Saw you not at the beginning of evening the antlered
    buck and his doe
Standing in the apple-orchard? I saw them. I saw them
    suddenly go,
Tails up, with long leaps lovely and slow,
Over the stone-wall into the wood of hemlocks bowed
    with snow.

Now lies he here, his wild blood scalding the snow.

How strange a thing is death, bringing to his knees,
    bringing to his antlers
The buck in the snow.
How strange a thing,—a mile away by now, it may be,
Under the heavy hemlocks that as the moments pass
Shift their loads a little, letting fall a feather of snow—
Life, looking out attentive from the eyes of the doe.

Evening on Lesbos

Twice having seen your shingled heads adorable
Side by side, the onyx and the gold,
I know that I have had what I could not hold.

Twice have I entered the room, not knowing she was here.
Two agate eyes, two eyes of malachite,
Twice have been turned upon me, hard and bright.

Whereby I know my loss.
                              Oh, not restorable
Sweet incense, mounting in the windless night!

Dirge Without Music

I am not resigned to the shutting away of loving hearts
      in the hard ground.
So it is, and so it will be, for so it has been, time out
      of mind:
Into the darkness they go, the wise and the lovely.
      Crowned
With lilies and with laurel they go; but I am not
      resigned.

Lovers and thinkers, into the earth with you.
Be one with the dull, the indiscriminate dust.
A fragment of what you felt, of what you knew,
A formula, a phrase remains,—but the best is lost.

The answers quick and keen, the honest look, the
      laughter, the love,—
They are gone. They are gone to feed the roses. Elegant
      and curled
Is the blossom. Fragrant is the blossom. I know. But I
      do not approve.
More precious was the light in your eyes than all the
      roses in the world.

Down, down, down into the darkness of the grave
Gently they go, the beautiful, the tender, the kind;
Quietly they go, the intelligent, the witty, the brave.
I know. But I do not approve. And I am not resigned.

Lethe

Ah, drink again
This river that is the taker-away of pain,
And the giver-back of beauty!

In these cool waves
What can be lost?—
Only the sorry cost
Of the lovely thing, ah, never the thing itself!

The level flood that laves
The hot brow
And the stiff shoulder
Is at our temples now.

Gone is the fever,
But not into the river;
Melted the frozen pride,
But the tranquil tide
Runs never the warmer for this,
Never the colder.

Immerse the dream.
Drench the kiss.
Dip the song in the stream.

To Inez Milholland

Read in Washington, November eighteenth, 1923, at the unveiling of a statue of three leaders in the cause of Equal Rights for Women

Upon this marble bust that is not I
Lay the round, formal wreath that is not fame;
But in the forum of my silenced cry
Root ye the living tree whose sap is flame.
I, that was proud and valiant, am no more;—
Save as a dream that wanders wide and late,
Save as a wind that rattles the stout door,
Troubling the ashes in the sheltered grate.
The stone will perish; I shall be twice dust.
Only my standard on a taken hill
Can cheat the mildew and the red-brown rust
And make immortal my adventurous will.
Even now the silk is tugging at the staff:
Take up the song; forget the epitaph.

To Jesus on His Birthday

For this your mother sweated in the cold,
For this you bled upon the bitter tree:
A yard of tinsel ribbon bought and sold;
A paper wreath; a day at home for me.
The merry bells ring out, the people kneel;
Up goes the man of God before the crowd;
With voice of honey and with eyes of steel
He drones your humble gospel to the proud.

Nobody listens. Less than the wind that blows
Are all your words to us you died to save.
O Prince of Peace! O Sharon's dewy Rose!
How mute you lie within your vaulted grave.
The stone the angel rolled away with tears
Is back upon your mouth these thousand years.

———

Not that it matters, not that my heart's cry
Is potent to deflect our common doom,
Or bind to truce in this ambiguous room
The planets of the atom as they ply;
But only to record that you and I,
Like thieves that scratch the jewels from a tomb,
Have gathered delicate love in hardy bloom
Close under Chaos,—I rise to testify.
This is my testament: that we are taken;
Our colours are as clouds before the wind;
Yet for a moment stood the foe forsaken,
Eyeing Love's favour to our helmet pinned;
Death is our master,—but his seat is shaken;
He rides victorious,—but his ranks are thinned.

ARIA DA CAPO | 1921

PERSONS

    PIERROT
    COLUMBINE
    COTHURNUS, MASQUE OF TRAGEDY
    THYRSIS   ⎫
           ⎬ SHEPHERDS
    CORYDON ⎭

SCENE: A STAGE

The curtain rises on a stage set for a Harlequinade, a merry black and white interior. Directly behind the footlights, and running parallel with them, is a long table, covered with a gay black and white cloth, on which is spread a banquet. At the opposite ends of this table, seated on delicate thin-legged chairs with high backs, are Pierrot and Columbine, dressed according to the tradition, excepting that Pierrot is in lilac, and Columbine in pink. They are dining.

COLUMBINE: Pierrot, a macaroon! I cannot *live*
  Without a macaroon!

PIERROT: My only love,
  You are *so* intense! . . . Is it Tuesday, Columbine?—
  I'll kiss you if it's Tuesday.

COLUMBINE: It is Wednesday,
  If you must know. . . . Is this my artichoke,
  Or yours?

PIERROT: Ah, Columbine,—as if it mattered!
   Wednesday. . . . Will it be Tuesday, then, to-morrow,
   By any chance?

COLUMBINE: To-morrow will be—Pierrot,
   That isn't funny!

PIERROT: I thought it rather nice.
   Well, let us drink some wine and lose our heads
   And love each other.

COLUMBINE: Pierrot, don't you love
   Me now?

PIERROT: La, what a woman!—how should I know?
   Pour me some wine: I'll tell you presently.

COLUMBINE: Pierrot, do you know, I think you drink too
      much.

PIERROT: Yes, I dare say I do. . . . Or else too little.
   It's hard to tell. You see, I am always wanting
   A little more than what I have,—or else
   A little less. There's something wrong. My dear,
   How many fingers have you?

COLUMBINE: La, indeed,
   How should I know?—It always takes me one hand
   To count the other with. It's too confusing.
   Why?

PIERROT: Why?—I am a student, Columbine;
   And search into all matters.

COLUMBINE: La, indeed?—
   Count them yourself, then!

PIERROT: No. Or, rather, *nay*.
  'Tis of no consequence. . . . I am become
  A painter, suddenly,—and you impress me—
  Ah, yes!—six orange bull's-eyes, four green
      pin-wheels,
  And one magenta jelly-roll,—the title
  As follows: *Woman Taking in Cheese from Fire-Escape.*

COLUMBINE: Well, I like that! So that is all I've meant
  To you!

PIERROT: Hush! All at once I am become
  A pianist. I will image you in sound. . . .
  On a new scale. . . . Without tonality. . . .
  Vivace senza tempo senza tutto. . . .
  Title: *Uptown Express at Six O'Clock.*
  Pour me a drink.

COLUMBINE: Pierrot, you work too hard.
  You need a rest. Come on out into the garden,
  And sing me something sad.

PIERROT: Don't stand so near me!
  I am become a socialist. I love
  Humanity; but I hate people. Columbine,
  Put on your mittens, child; your hands are cold.

COLUMBINE: My hands are *not* cold!

PIERROT: Oh, I am sure they are.
  And you must have a shawl to wrap about you,
  And sit by the fire.

COLUMBINE: Why, I'll do no such thing!
  I'm hot as a spoon in a teacup!

PIERROT: Columbine,
I'm a philanthropist. I know I am,
Because I feel so restless. Do not scream,
Or it will be the worse for you!

COLUMBINE: Pierrot,
My vinaigrette! I cannot *live* without
My vinaigrette!

PIERROT: My only love, you are
So fundamental! . . . How would you like to be
An actress, Columbine?—I am become
Your manager.

COLUMBINE: Why, Pierrot, *I* can't act.

PIERROT: Can't act! Can't act! La, listen to the woman!
What's that to do with the price of furs?—You're
    blonde,
Are you not?—you have no education, have you?—
Can't act! You underrate yourself, my dear!

COLUMBINE: Yes, I suppose I do.

PIERROT: As for the rest,
I'll teach you how to cry, and how to die,
And other little tricks; and the house will love you.
You'll be a star by five o'clock . . . that is,
If you will let me pay for your apartment.

COLUMBINE: *Let* you?—well, that's a good one!
                                   Ha! Ha! Ha!
But why?

PIERROT: But why?—well, as to that, my dear,
  I cannot say. It's just a matter of form.

COLUMBINE: Pierrot, I'm getting tired of caviar
  And peacocks' livers. Isn't there something else
  That people eat?—some humble vegetable,
  That grows in the ground?

PIERROT: Well, there are mushrooms.

COLUMBINE: Mushrooms!
  That's so! I had forgotten . . . mushrooms . . .
    mushrooms. . . .
  I cannot *live* with . . . How do you like this gown?

PIERROT: Not much. I'm tired of gowns that have the
    waist-line
  About the waist, and the hem around the bottom,—
  And women with their breasts in front of them!—
  Zut and ehè! Where does one go from here!

COLUMBINE: Here's a persimmon, love. You always liked
    them.

PIERROT: I am become a critic; there is nothing
  I can enjoy. . . . However, set it aside;
  I'll eat it between meals.

COLUMBINE: Pierrot, do you know,
  Sometimes I think you're making fun of me.

PIERROT: My love, by yon black moon, you wrong us
    both.

COLUMBINE: There isn't a sign of a moon, Pierrot.

PIERROT: Of course not.
　　There never was. "Moon's" just a word to swear by.
　　"Mutton!"—now *there's* a thing you can lay the
　　　　hands on,
　　And set the tooth in! Listen, Columbine:
　　I always lied about the moon and you.
　　Food is my only lust.

COLUMBINE: Well, eat it, then,
　　For Heaven's sake, and stop your silly noise!
　　I haven't heard the clock tick for an hour.

PIERROT: It's ticking all the same. If you were a fly,
　　You would be dead by now. And if I were a parrot,
　　I could be talking for a thousand years!

　　(*Enter* COTHURNUS.)

PIERROT: Hello, what's this, for God's sake?—
　　What's the matter?
　　Say, whadda you mean?—get off the stage, my friend,
　　And pinch yourself,—you're walking in your sleep!

COTHURNUS: I never sleep.

PIERROT: Well, anyhow, clear out.
　　You don't belong on here. Wait for your own scene!
　　Whadda you think this is,—a dress-rehearsal?

COTHURNUS: Sir, I am tired of waiting. I will wait
　　No longer.

PIERROT: Well, but whadda you going to do?
　　The scene is set for me!

COTHURNUS: True, sir; yet I
Can play the scene.

PIERROT: Your scene is down for later!

COTHURNUS: That, too, is true, sir; but I play it now.

PIERROT: Oh, very well!—Anyway, I am tired
Of black and white. At least, I think I am.

(*Exit* COLUMBINE.)

Yes, I am sure I am. I know what I'll do!—
I'll go and strum the moon, that's what I'll do. . . .
Unless, perhaps . . . you never can tell . . . I may be,
You know, tired of the moon. Well, anyway,
I'll go find Columbine. . . . And when I find her,
I will address her thus: "*Ehè*, Pierrette!"—
There's something in that.

(*Exit* PIERROT.)

COTHURNUS: You, Thyrsis! Corydon!
Where are you?

THYRSIS: (*Off stage.*) Sir, we are in our dressing-room!

COTHURNUS: Come out and do the scene.

CORYDON: (*Off stage.*) You are mocking us!—
The scene is down for later.

COTHURNUS: That is true;
But we will play it now. I am the scene.
(*Seats himself on high place in back of stage.*)

(*Enter* CORYDON *and* THYRSIS.)

CORYDON: Sir, we are counting on this little hour.
 We said, "Here is an hour,—in which to think
 A mighty thought, and sing a trifling song,
 And look at nothing."—And, behold! the hour,
 Even as we spoke, was over, and the act begun,
 Under our feet!

THYRSIS: Sir, we are not in the fancy
 To play the play. We had thought to play it later.

CORYDON: Besides, this is the setting for a farce.
 Our scene requires a wall; we cannot build
 A wall of tissue-paper!

THYRSIS: We cannot act
 A tragedy with comic properties!

COTHURNUS: Try it and see. I think you'll find you can.
 One wall is like another. And regarding
 The matter of your insufficient mood,
 The important thing is that you speak the lines,
 And make the gestures. Wherefore I shall remain
 Throughout, and hold the prompt-book. Are you
  ready?

CORYDON-THYRSIS: (*Sorrowfully.*) Sir, we are always
 ready.

COTHURNUS: Play the play!

 (CORYDON *and* THYRSIS *move the table and
 chairs to one side out of the way, and seat themselves
 in a half-reclining position on the floor.*)

THYRSIS: How gently in the silence, Corydon,
    Our sheep go up the bank. They crop a grass
    That's yellow where the sun is out, and black
    Where the clouds drag their shadows. Have you
        noticed
    How steadily, yet with what a slanting eye
    They graze?

CORYDON: As if they thought of other things.
    What say you, Thyrsis, do they only question
    Where next to pull?—Or do their far minds draw
        them
    Thus vaguely north of west and south of east?

THYRSIS: One cannot say. . . . The black lamb wears its
        burdocks
    As if they were a garland,—have you noticed?
    Purple and white—and drinks the bitten grass
    As if it were a wine.

CORYDON: I've noticed that.
    What say you, Thyrsis, shall we make a song
    About a lamb that thought himself a shepherd?

THYRSIS: Why, yes!—that is, why,—no. (I have
        forgotten my line.)

COTHURNUS: (*Prompting.*) "I know a game worth two of
        that!"

THYRSIS: Oh, yes. . . . I know a game worth two of that!
    Let's gather rocks, and build a wall between us;
    And say that over there belongs to me,
    And over here to you!

CORYDON: Why,—very well.
And say you may not come upon my side
Unless I say you may!

THYRSIS: Nor you on mine!
And if you should, 'twould be the worse for you!

(*They weave a wall of colored crêpe paper ribbons
from the centre front to the centre back of the stage,
fastening the ends to* COLUMBINE'S *chair in
front and to* PIERROT'S *chair in the back.*)

CORYDON: Now there's a wall a man may see across,
But not attempt to scale.

THYRSIS: An excellent wall.

CORYDON: Come, let us separate, and sit alone
A little while, and lay a plot whereby
We may outdo each other. (*They seat themselves on op-
posite sides of the wall.*)

PIERROT: (*Off stage.*) Ehè, Pierrette!

COLUMBINE: (*Off stage.*) My name is Columbine!
Leave me alone!

THYRSIS: (*Coming up to the wall.*)
Corydon, after all, and in spite of the fact
I started it myself, I do not like this
So very much. What is the sense of saying
I do not want you on my side the wall?
It is a silly game. I'd much prefer
Making the little song you spoke of making,

About the lamb, you know, that thought himself
A shepherd!—what do you say?

(*Pause.*)

CORYDON: (*At wall.*) (I have forgotten the line.)

COTHURNUS: (*Prompting.*) "How do I know this isn't a
trick?"

CORYDON: Oh, yes. . . . How do I know this isn't a trick
To get upon my land?

THYRSIS: Oh, Corydon,
You *know* it's not a trick. I do not like
The game, that's all. Come over here, or let me
Come over there.

CORYDON: It is a clever trick
To get upon my land. (*Seats himself as before.*)

THYRSIS: Oh, very well! (*Seats himself as before.*)
(*To himself.*) I think I never knew a sillier game.

CORYDON: (*Coming to wall.*)
Oh, Thyrsis, just a minute!—all the water
Is on your side the wall, and the sheep are thirsty.
I hadn't thought of that.

THYRSIS: Oh, hadn't you?

CORYDON: Why, what do you mean?

THYRSIS: What do I mean?—I mean
That I can play a game as well as you can.
And if the pool is on my side, it's on
My side, that's all.

CORYDON:　　　　　　　You mean you'd let the sheep
　Go thirsty?

THYRSIS:　Well, they're not my sheep. My sheep
　Have water enough.

CORYDON:　*Your* sheep! You are mad, to call them
　Yours—mine—they are all one flock! Thyrsis, you
　　can't mean
　To keep the water from them, just because
　They happened to be grazing over here
　Instead of over there, when we set the wall up?

THYRSIS:　Oh, can't I—wait and see!—and if you try
　To lead them over here, you'll wish you hadn't!

CORYDON:　I wonder how it happens all the water
　Is on your side. . . . I'll say you had an eye out
　For lots of little things, my innocent friend,
　When I said, "Let us make a song," and you said,
　"I know a game worth two of that!"

COLUMBINE:　(*Off stage.*)　　　　　　　Pierrot,
　D'you know, I think you must be getting old,
　Or fat, or something,—stupid, anyway!—
　Can't you put on some other kind of collar?

THYRSIS:　You know as well as I do, Corydon,
　I never thought anything of the kind.
　Don't you?

CORYDON:　　　　　　　　　　　　I *do* not.

THYRSIS:　　　　　　　　　　　Don't you?

CORYDON: Oh, I suppose so.
  Thyrsis, let's drop this,—what do you say?—it's only
  A game, you know . . . we seem to be forgetting
  It's only a game . . . a pretty serious game
  It's getting to be, when one of us is willing
  To let the sheep go thirsty for the sake of it.

THYRSIS: I know it, Corydon.

  (*They reach out their arms to each other across
  the wall.*)

COTHURNUS: (*Prompting.*) "But how do I know——"

THYRSIS: Oh, yes. . . . But how do I know this isn't a
    trick
  To water your sheep, and get the laugh on me?

CORYDON: You can't know, that's the difficult thing
    about it,
  Of course,—you can't be sure. You have to take
  My word for it. And I know just how you feel.
  But one of us has to take a risk, or else,
  Why, don't you see?—the game goes on forever! . . .
  It's terrible, when you stop to think of it. . . .
  Oh, Thyrsis, now for the first time I feel
  This wall is actually a wall, a thing
  Come up between us, shutting you away
  From me. . . . I do not know you any more!

THYRSIS: No, don't say that! Oh, Corydon, I'm willing
  To drop it all, if you will! Come on over
  And water your sheep! It is an ugly game.
  I hated it from the first. . . . How did it start?

CORYDON: I do not know . . . I do not know . . . I think
I am afraid of you!—you are a stranger!
I never set eyes on you before! "Come over
And water my sheep," indeed!—They'll be more thirsty
Than they are now before I bring them over
Into your land, and have you mixing them up
With yours, and calling them yours, and trying to
keep them!

(*Enter* COLUMBINE)

COLUMBINE: (*To* COTHURNUS.) Glummy, I want
my hat.

THYRSIS: Take it, and go.

COLUMBINE: Take it and go, indeed. Is it my hat,
Or isn't it? Is this my scene, or not?
Take it and go! Really, you know, you two
Are awfully funny!

(*Exit* COLUMBINE)

THYRSIS: Corydon, my friend,
I'm going to leave you now, and whittle me
A pipe, or sing a song, or go to sleep.
When you have come to your senses, let me know.

(*Goes back to where he has been sitting, lies down
and sleeps.*)

(CORYDON, *in going back to where he has been
sitting, stumbles over bowl of colored confetti and
colored paper ribbons.*)

CORYDON: Why, what is this?—Red stones—and purple
    stones—
  And stones stuck full of gold!—The ground is full
  Of gold and colored stones! . . . I'm glad the wall
  Was up before I found them!—Otherwise,
  I should have had to share them. As it is,
  They all belong to me. . . . Unless— (*He goes to wall
    and digs up and down the length of it, to see if there are
    jewels on the other side.*) None here——
  None here—none here— They all belong to me!
  (*Sits.*)

THYRSIS: (*Awakening.*) How curious! I thought the little
    black lamb
  Came up and licked my hair; I saw the wool
  About its neck as plain as anything!
  It must have been a dream. The little black lamb
  Is on the other side of the wall, I'm sure. (*Goes to wall
    and looks over.* CORYDON *is seated on the ground,
    tossing the confetti up into the air and catching it.*)
  Hello, what's that you've got there, Corydon?

CORYDON: Jewels.

THYRSIS: Jewels?—And where did you ever get them?

CORYDON: Oh, over here.

THYRSIS: You mean to say you found them,
  By digging around in the ground for them?

CORYDON: (*Unpleasantly.*)   No, Thyrsis,
  By digging down for water for my sheep.

THYRSIS: Corydon, come to the wall a minute, will you?
  I want to talk to you.

CORYDON: I haven't time.
  I'm making me a necklace of red stones.

THYRSIS: I'll give you all the water that you want,
  For one of those red stones,—if it's a good one.

CORYDON: Water?—what for?—what do I want of water?

THYRSIS: Why, for your sheep!

CORYDON: My sheep?—I'm not a shepherd!

THYRSIS: Your sheep are dying of thirst.

CORYDON: Man, haven't I told you
  I can't be bothered with a few untidy
  Brown sheep all full of burdocks?—I'm a merchant.
  That's what I am!—And if I set my mind to it
  I dare say I could be an emperor!
  (*To himself.*) Wouldn't I be a fool to spend my time
  Watching a flock of sheep go up a hill,
  When I have these to play with?—when I have these
  To think about?—I can't make up my mind
  Whether to buy a city, and have a thousand
  Beautiful girls to bathe me, and be happy
  Until I die, or build a bridge, and name it
  The Bridge of Corydon,—and be remembered
  After I'm dead.

THYRSIS: Corydon, come to the wall,
  Won't you?—I want to tell you something.

CORYDON: Hush!
  Be off! Be off! Go finish your nap, I tell you!

THYRSIS: Corydon, listen: if you don't want your sheep,
  Give them to me.

CORYDON: Be off! Go finish your nap.
  A red one—and a blue one—and a red one—
  And a purple one—give you my sheep, did you say?—
  Come, come! What do you take me for, a fool?
  I've a lot of thinking to do,—and while I'm thinking,
  The sheep might just as well be over here
  As over there. . . . A blue one—and a red one—

THYRSIS: But they will die!

CORYDON: And a green one—and a couple
  Of white ones, for a change.

THYRSIS: Maybe I have
  Some jewels on my side.

CORYDON: And another green one—
  Maybe, but I don't think so. You see, this rock
  Isn't so very wide. It stops before
  It gets to the wall. It seems to go quite deep,
  However.

THYRSIS: (*With hatred.*)   I see.

COLUMBINE: (*Off stage.*) Look, Pierrot, there's the moon.

PIERROT: (*Off stage.*) Nonsense!

THYRSIS: I see.

COLUMBINE: (*Off stage.*) Sing me an old song, Pierrot,—
Something I can remember.

PIERROT: (*Off stage.*)   Columbine.
Your mind is made of crumbs,—like an escallop
Of oysters,—first a layer of crumbs, and then
An oystery taste, and then a layer of crumbs.

THYRSIS: (*Searching.*) I find no jewels . . . but I wonder what
The root of this black weed would do to a man
If he should taste it. . . . I have seen a sheep die,
With half the stalk still drooling from its mouth.
'Twould be a speedy remedy, I should think,
For a festered pride and a feverish ambition.
It has a curious root. I think I'll hack it
In little pieces. . . . First I'll get me a drink;
And then I'll hack that root in little pieces
As small as dust, and see what the color is
Inside. (*Goes to bowl on floor.*)
              The pool is very clear. I see
A shepherd standing on the brink, with a red cloak
About him, and a black weed in his hand. . . .
'Tis I. (*Kneels and drinks.*)

CORYDON: (*Coming to wall.*) Hello, what are you doing,
Thyrsis?

THYRSIS: Digging for gold.

CORYDON: I'll give you all the gold
You want, if you'll give me a bowl of water.
If you don't want too much, that is to say.

THYRSIS: Ho, so you've changed your mind?—It's different,
    Isn't it, when you want a drink yourself?

CORYDON: Of course it is.

THYRSIS: Well, let me see . . . a bowl
    Of water,—come back in an hour, Corydon.
    I'm busy now.

CORYDON: Oh, Thyrsis, give me a bowl
    Of water!—and I'll fill the bowl with jewels,
    And bring it back!

THYRSIS: Be off, I'm busy now.

    (*He catches sight of the weed, picks it up and looks at it, unseen by* CORYDON.)

Wait!—Pick me out the finest stones you have . . .
    I'll bring you a drink of water presently.

CORYDON: (*Goes back and sits down, with the jewels before him.*)
    A bowl of jewels is a lot of jewels.

THYRSIS: (*Chopping up the weed.*) I wonder if it has a bitter taste.

CORYDON: There's sure to be a stone or two among them
    I have grown fond of, pouring them from one hand
    Into the other.

THYRSIS: I hope it doesn't taste
    Too bitter, just at first.

CORYDON: A bowl of jewels
    Is far too many jewels to give away
    And not get back again.

THYRSIS: I don't believe
    He'll notice. He's too thirsty. He'll gulp it down
    And never notice.

CORYDON: There ought to be some way
    To get them back again. . . . I could give him a
        necklace,
    And snatch it back, after I'd drunk the water,
    I suppose. . . . Why, as for that, of course a
    necklace. . . .

    (*He puts two or three of the colored tapes together
    and tries their strength by pulling them, after which
    he puts them around his neck and pulls them,
    gently, nodding to himself. He gets up and goes to the
    wall, with the colored tapes in his hands.*)

    (THYRSIS *in the meantime has poured the pow-
    dered root—black confetti—into the pot which con-
    tained the flower and filled it up with wine from the
    punch-bowl on the floor. He comes to the wall at the
    same time, holding the bowl of poison.*)

THYRSIS: Come, get your bowl of water, Corydon.

CORYDON: Ah, very good!—and for such a gift as that
    I'll give you more than a bowl of unset stones.
    I'll give you three long necklaces, my friend.
    Come closer. Here they are. (*Puts the ribbons about
        THYRSIS' neck.*)

THYRSIS: (*Putting bowl to* CORYDON'S *mouth.*)

I'll hold the bowl
Until you've drunk it all.

CORYDON: Then hold it steady.
For every drop you spill I'll have a stone back
Out of this chain.

THYRSIS: I shall not spill a drop.

(CORYDON *drinks, meanwhile beginning to
strangle* THYRSIS.)

THYRSIS: Don't pull the string so tight.

CORYDON: You're spilling the water.

THYRSIS: You've had enough—you've had enough—
    stop pulling
The string so tight!

CORYDON: Why, that's not tight at all . . .
How's this?

THYRSIS: (*Drops bowl.*) You're strangling me! Oh,
    Corydon!
It's only a game!—and you are strangling me!

CORYDON: It's only a game, is it?—Yet I believe
You've poisoned me in earnest! (*Writhes and pulls the
    strings tighter, winding them about* THYRSIS' *neck.*)

THYRSIS: Corydon! (*Dies.*)

CORYDON: You've poisoned me in earnest. . . . I feel
    so cold. . . .

So cold . . . this is a very silly game. . . .
Why do we play it?—let's not play this game
A minute more . . . let's make a little song
About a lamb. . . . I'm coming over the wall,
No matter what you say,—I want to be near you. . . .

(*Groping his way, with arms wide before him, he strides through the frail papers of the wall without knowing it, and continues seeking for the wall straight across the stage.*)

Where is the wall? (*Gropes his way back, and stands very near* THYRSIS *without seeing him; he speaks slowly.*)
                           There isn't any wall,
I think. (*Takes a step forward, his foot touches* THYRSIS' *body, and he falls down beside him.*)
Thyrsis, where is your cloak?—just give me
A little bit of your cloak! . . . (*Draws corner of* THYRSIS' *cloak over his shoulders, falls across* THYRSIS' *body, and dies.*)

(COTHURNUS *closes the prompt-book with a bang, arises matter-of-factly, comes down stage, and places the table over the two bodies, drawing down the cover so that they are hidden from any actors on the stage, but visible to the audience, pushing in their feet and hands with his boot. He then turns his back to the audience, and claps his hands twice.*)

COTHURNUS: Strike the scene! (*Exit* COTHURNUS.)

(*Enter* PIERROT *and* COLUMBINE.)

PIERROT: Don't puff so, Columbine!

COLUMBINE: Lord, what a mess
  This set is in! If there's one thing I hate
  Above everything else,—even more than getting my
    feet wet—
  It's clutter!—He might at least have left the scene
  The way he found it . . . don't you say so, Pierrot?

  (*She picks up punch bowl. They arrange chairs as
  before at ends of table.*)

PIERROT: Well, I don't know. I think it rather diverting
  The way it is. (*Yawns, picks up confetti bowl.*)
                                   Shall we begin?

COLUMBINE: (*Screams.*)   My God!
  What's that there under the table?

PIERROT: It is the bodies
  Of the two shepherds from the other play.

COLUMBINE: (*Slowly.*) How curious to strangle him like
    that,
  With colored paper ribbons.

PIERROT: Yes, and yet
  I dare say he is just as dead. (*Pauses. Calls.*) Cothurnus!
  Come drag these bodies out of here! We can't
  Sit down and eat with two dead bodies lying
  Under the table! . . . The audience wouldn't stand
    for it!

COTHURNUS: (*Off stage.*) What makes you think so?—
  Pull down the tablecloth
  On the other side, and hide them from the house,
  And play the farce. The audience will forget.

PIERROT: That's so. Give me a hand there, Columbine.

(PIERROT *and* COLUMBINE *pull down the table
cover in such a way that the two bodies are hidden
from the house, then merrily set their bowls back on
the table, draw up their chairs, and begin the play
exactly as before.*)

COLUMBINE: Pierrot, a macaroon,—I cannot *live*
Without a macaroon!

PIERROT: My only love,
You are *so* intense! . . . Is it Tuesday, Columbine?—
I'll kiss you if it's Tuesday. (*Curtains begin to close
slowly.*)

COLUMBINE: It is Wednesday,
If you must know. . . . Is this my artichoke
Or yours?

PIERROT: Ah, Columbine, as if it mattered!
Wednesday. . . . Will it be Tuesday, then, to-morrow,
By any chance? . . .

[CURTAIN.]

Ælfrida's Song

White-thorn and black-thorn,
Red haws in the hedge,
Sloes in the hedge, woad-black,
And a dusty dew on them;
Hairy stem
Of fennel,
Holy-bough and dill,
Dark yew;
Wormwood, woody nightshade,
And thy baleful sister, too!
   Show me in dream, yet nothing dim,
   The shadow and the shape of him!
   All Hallows Eve is All Saints Morning!

Thousand-blossom, white and red,
Spikèd willow-grass, wading-arrow;
I will lay him on my bed,
And bind his wounds with yarrow;
White-thorn, black-thorn, holy-bough, speed-well,—
Bind his wounds with yarrow.
   All Hallows Eve is All Saints Morning!

Seeds of poppy, small and black,
Borne to mill upon my back,

Into little loaves I'll knead,
For to bake him sleepy-bread;
Lest he leave me, lest he rise and leave me.
White-thorn, black-thorn, holy-bough, poppy-seed,
Bake him sleepy-bread.
   All Hallows Eve is All Saints Morning!

Nettle, sheathe thy naughty smart,
Be of bristles callow;
Bind his heart upon my heart,
Withy of the sallow.
White-thorn, black-thorn, periwinkle, holy-bough,
Withy of the sallow!
   All Hallows Eve is All Saints Morning!

White-thorn and black-thorn,
Thorn-apple, rank and reeking;
He shall drink mandragora,
Rooted up a-shrieking!
Holy-bough, white-thorn, holy-bough, black-thorn,
Holy-bough,
Mandragora!
   All Hallows Eve is All Saints Morning!

Rise now in dream, yet nothing dim,
The shadow and the shape of him.

Love Scene

ÆTHELWOLD

(He turns and leans his forehead against the trunk of the tree by which he is standing. Presently he turns and looks at her.)

Thou—knowest thou aught of love, and how it taketh a man?

Thinkest thou I am in love with thee?

ÆLFRIDA

(Faintly)

I would it were so. . . .

ÆTHELWOLD

(Staring at her)

I must be near thee or die.

(He comes blindly toward her and takes her in his arms.)

ÆLFRIDA

I am lost. . . . I am swept out to sea. . . .

(She lifts her face to his. He kisses her. They stand for a moment embraced.)

How thou shakest!

Art thou a-cold, my dear?

ÆTHELWOLD

Yea . . . nay . . . I know not . . .

I am a tree in a storm. . . .

(He turns from her, clinging to her hand, and sinks down upon the fallen tree.)

How silken-soft thou art,—
Wonderful . . . wonderful. . . .
How camest thou thus unwounded through the brambly
    wood?—
The brambly world?
Look at me: I am woven all of sedges,
Like a rush mat.

ÆLFRIDA
Not so.
    (*She spreads her cloak hastily over the log and seats
    herself upon it beside him. She touches his cheek.*)
Thy cheek is brown and smooth,
Like the rind of a nut
New bursten from his burr.
I have not seen thy like.

ÆTHELWOLD
The like of thee
Sings not nor blossoms.

The wind that soughs in the sedges at the edge of the
    pool
Has seen the swan go by,
So still and slow
And cool.

The bee that ferries his hoard from blossom to hive
Ere summer day be done,
Knows the sweet reek of the clover
Bruised by the wheels of the sun.

Wan ghost between
Two lights, the shadowy flutter-mouse,
Half-seeing and half-seen,
Swoops in the glimmering even;
The early star he knows,
And her cool wave upon his ribby fin.

Sweet, sweet,
Without, within,
Is the rose,
Whither the white moth steereth his sail.

Yet, ah, not wind nor bee
Nor any earthly wight
Hath seen what I see,
Nor hath any man heard from his father's father in an
    old tale
The like of thee.

ÆLFRIDA
Ah, me, how frosty sweet the moonlight!

ÆTHELWOLD
Icy sweet on thy mouth of ripened haws the
    moonlight. . . .
Belovèd . . . belovèd. . . .

ÆLFRIDA
Oh, darling head, shut out the moonlight from my
    mouth,
And kiss me in thy shadow!

ÆTHELWOLD

Drink, drink in haste my breath,
Ere it be swallowed up by thievish Death!
>   (*He kisses her. Presently her head falls back against
>   his shoulder.*)

ÆLFRIDA
>   (*Drowsily*)

O moon, draw not aside thy hem from this green moss
Ever, ever.

O droning Weird, let now thy busy spindle be at rest,
And do thou sleep awhile,
Thy shaggy head fallen forward upon thy breast.

O deep wood, unstill with small sounds,
Be kinsman to our love.
Nor let the chilly frost with his hoar rime
Creep up, creep up upon the drowsy summer
For yet a little time.

And ye, oak and beech,
With your dark boughs outspread,
Drop not your leaves, however shrunk and sere,
Upon a lover's hand, a lover's head.

Ere we find speech
For all this ache and wonder,
Oh, gast us not with the death of the year!
>   (*Suddenly she puts her arms about* ÆTHELWOLD'*s
>   neck and shrinks against him.*)
Ah, love, I fear a little, I fear, I fear

This fire we so recklessly kindled alone in the woods at
     night!
Hungry, hungry about us on every hand
It leaps and spreads among the trees!
Far off in the deep wood the grazing stag,
With listening hoof and antlers high,
Stands now with blinded eyes ablaze,
Bewildered in its light!

I love thee so! I love thee so!
     (*She takes his face in her hands and kisses him.
     Then sleepily, once more, her head falls back against
     his shoulder.*)

ÆTHELWOLD
Ah, could we hide us here in a cleft of the night,
And never be found!

ÆLFRIDA
Lost, lost,
Forgotten and lost,
Out of sight, out of sound!

ÆTHELWOLD
Letting the sun ride by, with his golden helmet,
And all his flashing spears and his flags out-streaming,—
Ride by, ride by, ride by,
Shaking the ground!

ÆLFRIDA
And never be found!

ÆTHELWOLD
Letting the world ride by, jingling his pennies
And telling his beads;
Time, drawn by the snail and the hare,
Asleep in his rattling wain;
Sorrow, giving her horse his head,
Riding in the rain;
Death, bloody-spurred,
Astride his iron bird!—

ÆLFRIDA
Ride by, ride by, ride by,
And never be found!

ÆTHELWOLD
Lost . . . lost. . . .

ÆLFRIDA
Forgotten and lost. . . .

ÆTHELWOLD
Out of sight. . . .

ÆLFRIDA
Out of sound. . . .
> (*Her head is on his shoulder. Her eyes are closed.*
> *They remain so for a moment, silent.*)

The Fang

No man that's worthy of the name
But in his helpless heart alive
Harbours a yellow, talkative
Serpent, he cannot hush nor tame.

Gaze if you like into the eyes
Of dryads. . . . Just before you drown,
The Fang says, "You've a date in town."

Beget your children, plant your trees,
Chisel your marble, build your song. . . .
The Fang says, "Well,—it's not for long."

Hope—if you're hopeful—or despair;
Nothing's to hinder you; but hark!—
Always the hissing head is there,
The insupportable remark.

Parisian Dream

I

That marvellous landscape of my dream—
Which no eye knows, nor ever will—
At moments, wide awake, I seem
To grasp, and it excites me still.

Sleep, how miraculous you are—
A strange caprice had urged my hand
To banish, as irregular,
All vegetation from that land;

And, proud of what my art had done,
I viewed my painting, knew the great
Intoxicating monotone
Of marble, water, steel and slate.

Staircases and arcades there were
In a long labyrinth, which led
To a vast palace; fountains there
Were gushing gold, and gushing lead.

And many a heavy cataract
Hung like a curtain,—did not fall,
As water does, but hung, compact,
Crystal, on many a metal wall.

Tall nymphs with Titan breasts and knees
Gazed at their images unblurred,
Where groves of colonnades, not trees,
Fringed a deep pool where nothing stirred.

Blue sheets of water, left and right,
Spread between quays of rose and green,
To the world's end and out of sight,
And still expanded, though unseen.

Enchanted rivers, those—with jade
And jasper were their banks bedecked;
Enormous mirrors, dazzled, made
Dizzy by all they did reflect.

And many a Ganges, taciturn
And heedless, in the vaulted air,
Poured out the treasure of its urn
Into a gulf of diamond there.

As architect, it tempted me
To tame the ocean at its source;
And this I did,—I made the sea
Under a jeweled culvert course.

And every colour, even black,
Became prismatic, polished, bright;
The liquid gave its glory back
Mounted in iridescent light.

There was no moon, there was no sun,—
For why should sun and moon conspire
To light such prodigies?—each one
Blazed with its own essential fire!

A silence like eternity
Prevailed, there was no sound to hear;
These marvels all were for the eye,
And there was nothing for the ear.

II

I woke; my mind was bright with flame;
I saw the cheap and sordid hole
I live in, and my cares all came
Burrowing back into my soul.

Brutally the twelve strokes of noon
Against my naked ear were hurled;
And a grey sky was drizzling down
Upon this sad, lethargic world.

Invitation to the Voyage

Think, would it not be
Sweet to live with me
All alone, my child, my love?—
Sleep together, share
All things, in that fair
Country you remind me of?
Charming in the dawn
There, the half-withdrawn
Drenched, mysterious sun appears
In the curdled skies,
Treacherous as your eyes
Shining from behind their tears.

There, restraint and order bless
Luxury and voluptuousness.

We should have a room
        Never out of bloom:
Tables polished by the palm
        Of the vanished hours
        Should reflect rare flowers
In that amber-scented calm;
        Ceilings richly wrought,
        Mirrors deep as thought,
Walls with eastern splendour hung,—
        All should speak apart
        To the homesick heart
In its own dear native tongue.

There, restraint and order bless
Luxury and voluptuousness.

        See, their voyage past,
        To their moorings fast,
On the still canals asleep,
        These big ships; to bring
        You some trifling thing
They have braved the furious deep.
        —Now the sun goes down,
        Tinting dyke and town,
Field, canal, all things in sight,
        Hyacinth and gold;
        All that we behold
Slumbers in its ruddy light.

There, restraint and order bless
Luxury and voluptuousness.

The Old Servant

The servant that we had, you were so jealous of,
I think we might at least lay flowers on her grave.
Good creature, she's beneath the sod . . . and we're
    above;
The dead, poor things, what valid grievances they have!
And, when October comes, stripping the wood of leaves,
And round their marble slabs the wind of autumn grieves,
Surely, a living man must seem to the cold dead
Somewhat unfeeling, sound asleep in his warm bed,
While, gnawed by blacker dreams than any we have
    known—
Lovers, good conversation, every pleasure gone—
Old bones concerning which the worm has had his say,
They feel the heavy snows of winter drip away,
And years go by, and no-one from the sagging vase
Lifts the dried flowers to put fresh flowers in their place.

Some evening, when the whistling log begins to purr,
Supposing, in that chair, appeared the ghost of her;
Supposing, on some cold and blue December night,
I found her in my room, humble, half out of sight,
And thoughtful, having come from her eternal bed
To shield her grown-up child, to soothe his troubled head,
What could I find to say to the poor faithful soul,—
Seeing the tears beneath those sunken eyelids roll?

Late January

Pluviose, hating all that lives, and loathing me,
Distills his cold and gloomy rain and slops it down
Upon the pallid lodgers in the cemetery
Next door, and on the people shopping in the town.

My cat, for sheer discomfort, waves a sparsely-furred
And shabby tail incessantly on the tiled floor;
And, wandering sadly in the rain-spout, can be heard
The voice of some dead poet who had these rooms before.

The log is wet, and smokes; its hissing high lament
Mounts to the bronchial clock on the cracked mantel
        there;
While (heaven knows whose they were—some dropsical
        old maid's)

In a soiled pack of cards that reeks of dirty scent,
The handsome jack of hearts and the worn queen of
        spades
Talk in suggestive tones of their old love-affair.

The King of the Rainy Country

A rainy country this, that I am monarch of,—
A rich but powerless king, worn-out while yet a boy;
For whom in vain the falcon falls upon the dove;
Not even his starving people's groans can give him joy;

Scorning his tutors, loathing his spaniels, finding stale
His favourite jester's quips, yawning at the droll tale.
His bed, for all its *fleurs de lis*, looks like a tomb;
The ladies of the court, attending him, to whom
He, being a prince, is handsome, see him lying there
Cold as a corpse, and lift their shoulders in despair:
No garment they take off, no garter they leave on
Excites the gloomy eye of this young skeleton.
The royal alchemist, who makes him gold from lead,
The baser element from out the royal head
Cannot extract; nor can those Roman baths of blood,
For some so efficacious, cure the hebetude
Of him, along whose veins, where flows no blood at all,
For ever the slow waters of green Lethe crawl.

Mists and Rains

O ends of autumns, winters, springtimes deep in mud,
Seasons of drowsiness,—my love and gratitude
I give you, that have wrapped with mist my heart and
    brain
As with a shroud, and shut them in a tomb of rain.

In this wide land when coldly blows the bleak south-west
And weather-vanes at night grow hoarse on the house-
    crest,
Better than in the time when green things bud and grow
My mounting soul spreads wide its black wings of a crow.

The heart filled up with gloom, and to the falling sleet
Long since accustomed, finds no other thing more
      sweet—
O dismal seasons, queens of our sad climate crowned—

Than to remain always in your pale shadows drowned
(Unless it be, some dark night, kissing an unseen head,
To rock one's pain to sleep upon a hazardous bed.)

A Memory

All this was long ago, but I do not forget
Our small white house, between the city and the farms;
The Venus, the Pomona,—I remember yet
How in the leaves they hid their chipping plaster charms;
And the majestic sun at evening, setting late,
Behind the pane that broke and scattered his bright rays,
How like an open eye he seemed to contemplate
Our long and silent dinners with a curious gaze:
The while his golden beams, like tapers burning there,
Made splendid the serge curtains and the simple fare.

I

What thing is this that, built of salt and lime
And such dry motes as in the sunbeam show,
Has power upon me that do daily climb
The dustless air?—for whom those peaks of snow
Whereup the lungs of man with borrowed breath
Go labouring to a doom I may not feel,
Are but a pearled and roseate plain beneath
My wingèd helmet and my wingèd heel.
What sweet emotions neither foe nor friend
Are these that clog my flight? what thing is this
That hastening headlong to a dusty end
Dare turn upon me these proud eyes of bliss?
Up, up, my feathers!—ere I lay you by
To journey barefoot with a mortal joy.

II

This beast that rends me in the sight of all,
This love, this longing, this oblivious thing,
That has me under as the last leaves fall,
Will glut, will sicken, will be gone by spring.
The wound will heal, the fever will abate,
The knotted hurt will slacken in the breast;
I shall forget before the flickers mate
Your look that is today my east and west.
Unscathed, however, from a claw so deep

Though I should love again I shall not go:
Along my body, waking while I sleep,
Sharp to the kiss, cold to the hand as snow,
The scar of this encounter like a sword
Will lie between me and my troubled lord.

III

No lack of counsel from the shrewd and wise
How love may be acquired and how conserved
Warrants this laying bare before your eyes
My needle to your north abruptly swerved;
If I would hold you, I must hide my fears
Lest you be wanton, lead you to believe
My compass to another quarter veers,
Little surrender, lavishly receive.
But being like my mother the brown earth
Fervent and full of gifts and free from guile,
Liefer would I you loved me for my worth,
Though you should love me but a little while,
Than for a philtre any doll can brew,—
Though thus I bound you as I long to do.

IV

Nay, learnèd doctor, these fine leeches fresh
From the pond's edge my cause cannot remove:
Alas, the sick disorder in my flesh
Is deeper than your skill, is very love.
And you, good friar, far liefer would I think
Upon my dear, and dream him in your place,
Than heed your *ben'cites* and heavenward sink
With empty heart and noddle full of grace.

Breathes but one mortal on the teeming globe
Could minister to my soul's or body's needs—
Physician minus physic, minus robe;
Confessor minus Latin, minus beads.
Yet should you bid me name him, I am dumb;
For though you summon him, he would not come.

V

Of all that ever in extreme disease
"Sweet Love, sweet cruel Love, have pity!" cried,
Count me the humblest, hold me least of these
That wear the red heart crumpled in the side,
In heaviest durance, dreaming or awake,
Filling the dungeon with their piteous woe;
Not that I shriek not till the dungeon shake,
"Oh, God! Oh, let me out! Oh, let me go!"
But that my chains throughout their iron length
Make such a golden clank upon my ear,
But that I would not, boasted I the strength,
Up with a terrible arm and out of here
Where thrusts my morsel daily through the bars
This tall, oblivious gaoler eyed with stars.

VI

Since I cannot persuade you from this mood
Of pale preoccupation with the dead,
Not for my comfort nor for your own good
Shift your concern to living bones instead;
Since that which Helen did and ended Troy
Is more than I can do though I be warm;
Have up your buried girls, egregious boy,

And stand with them against the unburied storm.
When you lie wasted and your blood runs thin,
And what's to do must with dispatch be done,
Call Cressid, call Elaine, call Isolt in!—
More bland the ichor of a ghost should run
Along your dubious veins than the rude sea
Of passion pounding all day long in me.

VII

Night is my sister, and how deep in love,
How drowned in love and weedily washed ashore,
There to be fretted by the drag and shove
At the tide's edge, I lie—these things and more:
Whose arm alone between me and the sand,
Whose voice alone, whose pitiful breath brought near,
Could thaw these nostrils and unlock this hand,
She could advise you, should you care to hear.
Small chance, however, in a storm so black,
A man will leave his friendly fire and snug
For a drowned woman's sake, and bring her back
To drip and scatter shells upon the rug.
No one but Night, with tears on her dark face,
Watches beside me in this windy place.

VIII

Yet in an hour to come, disdainful dust,
You shall be bowed and brought to bed with me.
While the blood roars, or when the blood is rust
About a broken engine, this shall be.
If not today, then later; if not here
On the green grass, with sighing and delight,
Then under it, all in good time, my dear,

We shall be laid together in the night.
And ruder and more violent, be assured,
Than the desirous body's heat and sweat
That shameful kiss by more than night obscured
Wherewith at length the scornfullest mouth is met.
Life has no friend; her converts late or soon
Slide back to feed the dragon with the moon.

IX

When you are dead, and your disturbing eyes
No more as now their stormy lashes lift
To lance me through—as in the morning skies
One moment, plainly visible in a rift
Of cloud, two splendid planets may appear
And purely blaze, and are at once withdrawn,
What time the watcher in desire and fear
Leans from his chilly window in the dawn—
Shall I be free, shall I be once again
As others are, and count your loss no care?
Oh, never more, till my dissolving brain
Be powerless to evoke you out of air,
Remembered morning stars, more fiercely bright
Than all the Alphas of the actual night!

X

Strange thing that I, by nature nothing prone
To fret the summer blossom on its stem,
Who know the hidden nest, but leave alone
The magic eggs, the bird that cuddles them,
Should have no peace till your bewildered heart
Hung fluttering at the window of my breast,
Till I had ravished to my bitter smart

Your kiss from the stern moment, could not rest.
"Swift wing, sweet blossom, live again in air!
Depart, poor flower; poor feathers you are free!"
Thus do I cry, being teased by shame and care
That beauty should be brought to terms by me;
Yet shamed the more that in my heart I know,
Cry as I may, I could not let you go.

XI

Not in a silver casket cool with pearls
Or rich with red corundum or with blue,
Locked, and the key withheld, as other girls
Have given their loves, I give my love to you;
Not in a lovers'-knot, not in a ring
Worked in such fashion, and the legend plain—
Semper fidelis, where a secret spring
Kennels a drop of mischief for the brain:
Love in the open hand, no thing but that,
Ungemmed, unhidden, wishing not to hurt,
As one should bring you cowslips in a hat
Swung from the hand, or apples in her skirt,
I bring you, calling out as children do:
"Look what I have!—And these are all for you."

XII

Olympian gods, mark now my bedside lamp
Blown out; and be advised too late that he
Whom you call sire is stolen into the camp
Of warring Earth, and lies abed with me.
Call out your golden hordes, the harm is done:
Enraptured in his great embrace I lie;

Shake heaven with spears, but I shall bear a son
Branded with godhead, heel and brow and thigh.
Whom think not to bedazzle or confound
With meteoric splendours or display
Of blackened moons or suns or the big sound
Of sudden thunder on a silent day;
Pain and compassion shall he know, being mine,—
Confusion never, that is half divine.

XIII

I said, seeing how the winter gale increased,
Even as waxed within us and grew strong
The ancient tempest of desire, "At least,
It is the season when the nights are long.
Well flown, well shattered from the summer hedge
The early sparrow and the opening flowers!—
Late climbs the sun above the southerly edge
These days, and sweet to love those added hours."
Alas, already does the dark recede,
And visible are the trees against the snow.
Oh, monstrous parting, oh, perfidious deed,
How shall I leave your side, how shall I go? . . .
Unnatural night, the shortest of the year,
Farewell! 'Tis dawn. The longest day is here.

XIV

Since of no creature living the last breath
Is twice required, or twice the ultimate pain,
Seeing how to quit your arms is very death,
'Tis likely that I shall not die again;
And likely 'tis that Time whose gross decree

Sends now the dawn to clamour at our door,
Thus having done his evil worst to me,
Will thrust me by, will harry me no more.
When you are corn and roses and at rest
I shall endure, a dense and sanguine ghost,
To haunt the scene where I was happiest,
To bend above the thing I loved the most;
And rise, and wring my hands, and steal away
As I do now, before the advancing day.

xv

My worship from this hour the Sparrow-Drawn
Alone will cherish, and her arrowy child,
Whose groves alone in the inquiring dawn
Rise tranquil, and their altars undefiled.
Seaward and shoreward smokes a plundered land
To guard whose portals was my dear employ;
Razed are its temples now; inviolate stand
Only the slopes of Venus and her boy.
How have I stripped me of immortal aid
Save theirs alone,—who could endure to see
Forsworn Aeneas with conspiring blade
Sever the ship from shore (alas for me)
And make no sign; who saw, and did not speak,
The brooch of Troilus pinned upon the Greek.

xvi

I dreamed I moved among the Elysian fields,
In converse with sweet women long since dead;
And out of blossoms which that meadow yields
I wove a garland for your living head.

Danae, that was the vessel for a day
Of golden Jove, I saw, and at her side,
Whom Jove the Bull desired and bore away,
Europa stood, and the Swan's featherless bride.
All these were mortal women, yet all these
Above the ground had had a god for guest;
Freely I walked beside them and at ease,
Addressing them, by them again addressed,
And marvelled nothing, for remembering you,
Wherefore I was among them well I knew.

XVII

Sweet love, sweet thorn, when lightly to my heart
I took your thrust, whereby I since am slain,
And lie disheveled in the grass apart,
A sodden thing bedrenched by tears and rain,
While rainy evening drips to misty night,
And misty night to cloudy morning clears,
And clouds disperse across the gathering light,
And birds grow noisy, and the sun appears—
Had I bethought me then, sweet love, sweet thorn,
How sharp an anguish even at the best,
When all's requited and the future sworn,
The happy hour can leave within the breast,
I had not so come running at the call
Of one who loves me little, if at all.

XVIII

Shall I be prisoner till my pulses stop
To hateful Love and drag his noisy chain,
And bait my need with sugared crusts that drop

From jeweled fingers neither kind nor clean?—
Mewed in an airless cavern where a toad
Would grieve to snap his gnat and lay him down,
While in the light along the rattling road
Men shout and chaff and drive their wares to town? . . .
Perfidious Prince, that keep me here confined,
Doubt not I know the letters of my doom:
How many a man has left his blood behind
To buy his exit from this mournful room
These evil stains record, these walls that rise
Carved with his torment, steamy with his sighs.

XIX

My most distinguished guest and learnèd friend,
The pallid hare that runs before the day
Having brought your earnest counsels to an end
Now have I somewhat of my own to say:
That it is folly to be sunk in love,
And madness plain to make the matter known,
These are no mysteries you are verger of;
Everyman's wisdoms these are, and my own.
If I have flung my heart unto a hound
I have done ill, it is a certain thing;
Yet breathe I freer, walk I the more sound
On my sick bones for this brave reasoning?
Soon must I say, " 'Tis prowling Death I hear!"
Yet come no better off, for my quick ear.

XX

Think not, nor for a moment let your mind,
Wearied with thinking, doze upon the thought
That the work's done and the long day behind,

And beauty, since 'tis paid for, can be bought.
If in the moonlight from the silent bough
Suddenly with precision speak your name
The nightingale, be not assured that now
His wing is limed and his wild virtue tame.
Beauty beyond all feathers that have flown
Is free; you shall not hood her to your wrist,
Nor sting her eyes, nor have her for your own
In any fashion; beauty billed and kissed
Is not your turtle; tread her like a dove—
She loves you not; she never heard of love.

XXI

Gone in good sooth you are: not even in dream
You come. As if the strictures of the light,
Laid on our glances to their disesteem,
Extended even to shadows and the night;
Extended even beyond that drowsy sill
Along whose galleries open to the skies
All maskers move unchallenged and at will,
Visor in hand or hooded to the eyes.
To that pavilion the green sea in flood
Curves in, and the slow dancers dance in foam;
I find again the pink camellia-bud
On the wide step, beside a silver comb. . . .
But it is scentless; up the marble stair
I mount with pain, knowing you are not there.

XXII

Now by this moon, before this moon shall wane
I shall be dead or I shall be with you!
No moral concept can outweigh the pain

Past rack and wheel this absence puts me through;
Faith, honour, pride, endurance, what the tongues
Of tedious men will say, or what the law—
For which of these do I fill up my lungs
With brine and fire at every breath I draw?
Time, and to spare, for patience by and by,
Time to be cold and time to sleep alone;
Let me no more until the hour I die
Defraud my innocent senses of their own.
Before this moon shall darken, say of me:
She's in her grave, or where she wants to be.

XXIII

I know the face of Falsehood and her tongue
Honeyed with unction, plausible with guile,
Are dear to men, whom count me not among,
That owe their daily credit to her smile;
Such have been succoured out of great distress
By her contriving, if accounts be true:
Their deference now above the board, I guess,
Discharges what beneath the board is due.
As for myself, I'd liefer lack her aid
Than eat her presence; let this building fall:
But let me never lift my latch, afraid
To hear her simpering accents in the hall,
Nor force an entrance past mephitic airs
Of stale patchouli hanging on my stairs.

XXIV

Whereas at morning in a jeweled crown
I bit my fingers and was hard to please,
Having shook disaster till the fruit fell down

I feel tonight more happy and at ease:
Feet running in the corridors, men quick-
Buckling their sword-belts bumping down the stair,
Challenge, and rattling bridge-chain, and the click
Of hooves on pavement—this will clear the air.
Private this chamber as it has not been
In many a month of muffled hours; almost,
Lulled by the uproar, I could lie serene
And sleep, until all's won, until all's lost,
And the door's opened and the issue shown,
And I walk forth Hell's mistress . . . or my own.

XXV

Peril upon the paths of this desire
Lies like the natural darkness of the night,
For me unpeopled; let him hence retire
Whom as a child a shadow could affright;
And fortune speed him from this dubious place
Where roses blenched or blackened of their hue,
Pallid and stemless float on undulant space,
Or clustered hidden shock the hand with dew.
Whom as a child the night's obscurity
Did not alarm, let him alone remain,
Lanterned but by the longing in the eye,
And warmed but by the fever in the vein,
To lie with me, sentried from wrath and scorn
By sleepless Beauty and her polished thorn.

XXVI

Women have loved before as I love now;
At least, in lively chronicles of the past—
Of Irish waters by a Cornish prow

Or Trojan waters by a Spartan mast
Much to their cost invaded—here and there,
Hunting the amorous line, skimming the rest,
I find some woman bearing as I bear
Love like a burning city in the breast.
I think however that of all alive
I only in such utter, ancient way
Do suffer love; in me alone survive
The unregenerate passions of a day
When treacherous queens, with death upon the tread,
Heedless and wilful, took their knights to bed.

XXVII

Moon, that against the lintel of the west
Your forehead lean until the gate be swung,
Longing to leave the world and be at rest,
Being worn with faring and no longer young,
Do you recall at all the Carian hill
Where worn with loving, loving late you lay,
Halting the sun because you lingered still,
While wondering candles lit the Carian day?
Ah, if indeed this memory to your mind
Recall some sweet employment, pity me,
That with the dawn must leave my love behind,
That even now the dawn's dim herald see!
I charge you, goddess, in the name of one
You loved as well: endure, hold off the sun.

XXVIII

When we are old and these rejoicing veins
Are frosty channels to a muted stream,
And out of all our burning there remains
No feeblest spark to fire us, even in dream,
This be our solace: that it was not said
When we were young and warm and in our prime,
Upon our couch we lay as lie the dead,
Sleeping away the unreturning time.
O sweet, O heavy-lidded, O my love,
When morning strikes her spear upon the land,
And we must rise and arm us and reprove
The insolent daylight with a steady hand,
Be not discountenanced if the knowing know
We rose from rapture but an hour ago.

XXIX

Heart, have no pity on this house of bone:
Shake it with dancing, break it down with joy.
No man holds mortgage on it; it is your own;
To give, to sell at auction, to destroy.
When you are blind to moonlight on the bed,
When you are deaf to gravel on the pane,
Shall quavering caution from this house instead
Cluck forth at summer mischief in the lane?
All that delightful youth forbears to spend
Molestful age inherits, and the ground
Will have us; therefore, while we're young, my friend—
The Latin's vulgar, but the advice is sound.
Youth, have no pity; leave no farthing here
For age to invest in compromise and fear.

XXX

Love is not all: it is not meat nor drink
Nor slumber nor a roof against the rain;
Nor yet a floating spar to men that sink
And rise and sink and rise and sink again;
Love can not fill the thickened lung with breath,
Nor clean the blood, nor set the fractured bone;
Yet many a man is making friends with death
Even as I speak, for lack of love alone.
It well may be that in a difficult hour,
Pinned down by pain and moaning for release,
Or nagged by want past resolution's power,
I might be driven to sell your love for peace,
Or trade the memory of this night for food.
It well may be. I do not think I would.

XXXI

When we that wore the myrtle wear the dust,
And years of darkness cover up our eyes,
And all our arrogant laughter and sweet lust
Keep counsel with the scruples of the wise;
When boys and girls that now are in the loins
Of croaking lads, dip oar into the sea,—
And who are these that dive for copper coins?
No longer we, my love, no longer we—
Then let the fortunate breathers of the air,
When we lie speechless in the muffling mould,
Tease not our ghosts with slander, pause not there
To say that love is false and soon grows cold,
But pass in silence the mute grave of two
Who lived and died believing love was true.

XXXII

Time, that is pleased to lengthen out the day
For grieving lovers parted or denied,
And pleased to hurry the sweet hours away
From such as lie enchanted side by side,
Is not my kinsman; nay, my feudal foe
Is he that in my childhood was the thief
Of all my mother's beauty, and in woe
My father bowed, and brought our house to grief.
Thus, though he think to touch with hateful frost
Your treasured curls, and your clear forehead line,
And so persuade me from you, he has lost;
Never shall he inherit what was mine.
When Time and all his tricks have done their worst,
Still will I hold you dear, and him accurst.

XXXIII

Sorrowful dreams remembered after waking
Shadow with dolour all the candid day;
Even as I read, the silly tears out-breaking
Splash on my hands and shut the page away. . . .
Grief at the root, a dark and secret dolour,
Harder to bear than wind-and-weather grief,
Clutching the rose, draining its cheek of colour,
Drying the bud, curling the opened leaf.
Deep is the pond—although the edge be shallow,
Frank in the sun, revealing fish and stone,
Climbing ashore to turtle-head and mallow—
Black at the centre beats a heart unknown.
Desolate dreams pursue me out of sleep;
Weeping I wake; waking, I weep, I weep.

XXXIV

Most wicked words! forbear to speak them out.
Utter them not again; blaspheme no more
Against our love with maxims learned from Doubt:
Lest Death should get his foot inside the door.
We are surrounded by a hundred foes;
And he that at your bidding joins our feast,
I stake my heart upon it, is one of those,
Nor in their councils does he sit the least.
Hark not his whisper: he is Time's ally,
Kinsman to Death, and leman of Despair:
Believe that I shall love you till I die;
Believe; and thrust him forth; and arm the stair;
And top the walls with spikes and splintered glass
That he pass gutted should again he pass.

XXXV

Clearly my ruined garden as it stood
Before the frost came on it I recall—
Stiff marigolds, and what a trunk of wood
The zinnia had, that was the first to fall;
These pale and oozy stalks, these hanging leaves
Nerveless and darkened, dripping in the sun,
Cannot gainsay me, though the spirit grieves
And wrings its hands at what the frost has done.
If in a widening silence you should guess
I read the moment with recording eyes,
Taking your love and all your loveliness
Into a listening body hushed of sighs . . .
Though summer's rife and the warm rose in season,
Rebuke me not: I have a winter reason.

XXXVI

Hearing your words, and not a word among them
Tuned to my liking, on a salty day
When inland woods were pushed by winds that flung them
Hissing to leeward like a ton of spray,
I thought how off Matinicus the tide
Came pounding in, came running through the Gut,
While from the Rock the warning whistle cried,
And children whimpered, and the doors blew shut;
There in the autumn when the men go forth,
With slapping skirts the island women stand
In gardens stripped and scattered, peering north,
With dahlia tubers dripping from the hand:
The wind of their endurance, driving south,
Flattened your words against your speaking mouth.

XXXVII

Believe, if ever the bridges of this town,
Whose towers were builded without fault or stain,
Be taken, and its battlements go down,
No mortal roof shall shelter me again;
I shall not prop a branch against a bough
To hide me from the whipping east or north,
Nor tease to flame a heap of sticks, who now
Am warmed by all the wonders of the earth.
Do you take ship unto some happier shore
In such event, and have no thought for me,
I shall remain;—to share the ruinous floor
With roofs that once were seen far out at sea;
To cheer a mouldering army on the march . . .
And beg from spectres by a broken arch.

XXXVIII

You say: "Since life is cruel enough at best;"
You say: "Considering how our love is cursed,
And housed so bleakly that the sea-gull's nest
Were better shelter, even as better nursed
Between the breaker and the stingy reeds
Ragged and coarse that hiss against the sand
The gull's brown chick, and hushed in all his needs,
Than our poor love so harried through the land—
You being too tender, even with all your scorn,
To line his cradle with the world's reproof,
And I too devious, too surrendered, born
Too far from home to hunt him even a roof
Out of the rain—" Oh, tortured voice, be still!
Spare me your premise: leave me when you will.

XXXIX

Love me no more, now let the god depart,
If love be grown so bitter to your tongue!
Here is my hand; I bid you from my heart
Fare well, fare very well, be always young.
As for myself, mine was a deeper drouth:
I drank and thirsted still; but I surmise
My kisses now are sand against your mouth,
Teeth in your palm and pennies on your eyes.
Speak but one cruel word, to shame my tears;
Go, but in going, stiffen up my back
To meet the yelping of the mustering years—
Dim, trotting shapes that seldom will attack
Two with a light who match their steps and sing:
To one alone and lost, another thing.

XL

You loved me not at all, but let it go;
I loved you more than life, but let it be.
As the more injured party, this being so,
The hour's amenities are all to me—
The choice of weapons; and I gravely choose
To let the weapons tarnish where they lie;
And spend the night in eloquent abuse
Of senators and popes and such small fry
And meet the morning standing, and at odds
With heaven and earth and hell and any fool
Who calls his soul his own, and all the gods,
And all the children getting dressed for school . . .
And you will leave me, and I shall entomb
What's cold by then in an adjoining room.

XLI

I said in the beginning, did I not?—
Prophetic of the end, though unaware
How light you took me, ignorant that you thought
I spoke to see my breath upon the air:
If you walk east at daybreak from the town
To the cliff's foot, by climbing steadily
You cling at noon whence there is no way down
But to go toppling backward to the sea.
And not for birds nor birds'-eggs, so they say,
But for a flower that in these fissures grows,
Forms have been seen to move throughout the day
Skyward; but what its name is no one knows.
'Tis said you find beside them on the sand
This flower, relinquished by the broken hand.

XLII

O ailing Love, compose your struggling wing!
Confess you mortal; be content to die.
How better dead, than be this awkward thing
Dragging in dust its feathers of the sky;
Hitching and rearing, plunging beak to loam,
Upturned, disheveled, uttering a weak sound
Less proud than of the gull that rakes the foam,
Less kind than of the hawk that scours the ground.
While yet your awful beauty, even at bay,
Beats off the impious eye, the outstretched hand,
And what your hue or fashion none can say,
Vanish, be fled, leave me a wingless land . . .
Save where one moment down the quiet tide
Fades a white swan, with a black swan beside.

XLIII

Summer, be seen no more within this wood;
Nor you, red Autumn, down its paths appear;
Let no more the false mitrewort intrude
Nor the dwarf cornel nor the gentian here;
You too be absent, unavailing Spring,
Nor let those thrushes that with pain conspire
From out this wood their wild arpeggios fling,
Shaking the nerves with memory and desire.
Only that season which is no man's friend,
You, surly Winter, in this wood be found;
Freeze up the year; with sleet these branches bend
Though rasps the locust in the fields around.
Now darken, sky! Now shrieking blizzard, blow!—
Farewell, sweet bank; be blotted out with snow.

XLIV

If to be left were to be left alone,
And lock the door and find one's self again—
Drag forth and dust Penates of one's own
That in a corner all too long have lain;
Read Brahms, read Chaucer, set the chessmen out
In classic problem, stretch the shrunken mind
Back to its stature on the rack of thought—
Loss might be said to leave its boon behind.
But fruitless conference and the interchange
With callow wits of bearded *cons* and *pros*
Enlist the neutral daylight, and derange
A will too sick to battle for repose.
Neither with you nor with myself, I spend
Loud days that have no meaning and no end.

XLV

I know my mind and I have made my choice;
Not from your temper does my doom depend;
Love me or love me not, you have no voice
In this, which is my portion to the end.
Your presence and your favours, the full part
That you could give, you now can take away:
What lies between your beauty and my heart
Not even you can trouble or betray.
Mistake me not—unto my inmost core
I do desire your kiss upon my mouth;
They have not craved a cup of water more
That bleach upon the deserts of the south;
Here might you bless me; what you cannot do
Is bow me down, who have been loved by you.

XLVI

Even in the moment of our earliest kiss,
When sighed the straitened bud into the flower,
Sat the dry seed of most unwelcome this;
And that I knew, though not the day and hour.
Too season-wise am I, being country-bred,
To tilt at autumn or defy the frost:
Snuffing the chill even as my fathers did,
I say with them, "What's out tonight is lost."
I only hoped, with the mild hope of all
Who watch the leaf take shape upon the tree,
A fairer summer and a later fall
Than in these parts a man is apt to see,
And sunny clusters ripened for the wine:
I tell you this across the blackened vine.

XLVII

Well, I have lost you; and I lost you fairly;
In my own way, and with my full consent.
Say what you will, kings in a tumbrel rarely
Went to their deaths more proud than this one went.
Some nights of apprehension and hot weeping
I will confess; but that's permitted me;
Day dried my eyes; I was not one for keeping
Rubbed in a cage a wing that would be free.
If I had loved you less or played you slyly
I might have held you for a summer more,
But at the cost of words I value highly,
And no such summer as the one before.
Should I outlive this anguish—and men do—
I shall have only good to say of you.

XLVIII

Now by the path I climbed, I journey back.
The oaks have grown; I have been long away.
Taking with me your memory and your lack
I now descend into a milder day;
Stripped of your love, unburdened of my hope,
Descend the path I mounted from the plain;
Yet steeper than I fancied seems the slope
And stonier, now that I go down again.
Warm falls the dusk; the clanking of a bell
Faintly ascends upon this heavier air;
I do recall those grassy pastures well:
In early spring they drove the cattle there.
And close at hand should be a shelter, too,
From which the mountain peaks are not in view.

XLIX

There is a well into whose bottomless eye,
Though I were flayed, I dare not lean and look,
Sweet once with mountain water, now gone dry,
Miraculously abandoned by the brook
Wherewith for years miraculously fed
It kept a constant level cold and bright,
Though summer parched the rivers in their bed;
Withdrawn these waters, vanished overnight.
There is a word I dare not speak again,
A face I never again must call to mind;
I was not craven ever nor blenched at pain,
But pain to such degree and of such kind
As I must suffer if I think of you,
Not in my senses will I undergo.

L

The heart once broken is a heart no more,
And is absolved from all a heart must be;
All that it signed or chartered heretofore
Is cancelled now, the bankrupt heart is free;
So much of duty as you may require
Of shards and dust, this and no more of pain,
This and no more of hope, remorse, desire,
The heart once broken need support again.
How simple 'tis, and what a little sound
It makes in breaking, let the world attest:
It struggles, and it fails; the world goes round,
And the moon follows it. Heart in my breast,
'Tis half a year now since you broke in two;
The world's forgotten well, if the world knew.

LI

If in the years to come you should recall,
When faint at heart or fallen on hungry days,
Or full of griefs and little if at all
From them distracted by delights or praise;
When failing powers or good opinion lost
Have bowed your neck, should you recall to mind
How of all men I honoured you the most,
Holding you noblest among mortal-kind:
Might not my love—although the curving blade
From whose wide mowing none may hope to hide,
Me long ago below the frosts had laid—
Restore you somewhat to your former pride?
Indeed I think this memory, even then,
Must raise you high among the run of men.

Oh, sleep forever in the Latmian cave,
Mortal Endymion, darling of the Moon!
Her silver garments by the senseless wave
Shouldered and dropped and on the shingle strewn,
Her fluttering hand against her forehead pressed,
Her scattered looks that trouble all the sky,
Her rapid footsteps running down the west—
Of all her altered state, oblivious lie!
Whom earthen you, by deathless lips adored,
Wild-eyed and stammering to the grasses thrust,
And deep into her crystal body poured
The hot and sorrowful sweetness of the dust:
Whereof she wanders mad, being all unfit
For mortal love, that might not die of it.

IV

Valentine

Oh, what a shining town were Death
Woke you therein, and drew your breath,
My buried love; and all you were,
Caught up and cherished, even there.
Those evil windows loved of none
Would blaze as if they caught the sun.

Woke you in Heaven, Death's kinder name,
And downward in sweet gesture came
From your cold breast your rigid hand,
Then Heaven would be my native land.

But you are nowhere: you are gone
All roads into Oblivion.
Whither I would disperse, till then
From home a banished citizen.

In the Grave No Flower

Here dock and tare.
But there
No flower.

Here beggar-ticks, 'tis true;
Here the rank-smelling
Thorn-apple,—and who
Would plant this by his dwelling?
Here every manner of weed
To mock the faithful harrow:
Thistles, that feed
None but the finches; yarrow,
Blue vervain, yellow charlock; here
Bindweed, that chokes the struggling year;
Broad plantain and narrow.

But there no flower.

The rye is vexed and thinned,
The wheat comes limping home,
By vetch and whiteweed harried, and the sandy bloom
Of the sour-grass; here
Dandelions,—and the wind
Will blow them everywhere.

Save there.
There
No flower.

Childhood Is the Kingdom Where Nobody Dies

Childhood is not from birth to a certain age and at a
    certain age
The child is grown, and puts away childish things.
Childhood is the kingdom where nobody dies.

Nobody that matters, that is. Distant relatives of course
Die, whom one never has seen or has seen for an hour,
And they gave one candy in a pink-and-green stripèd
    bag, or a jack-knife,
And went away, and cannot really be said to have lived
    at all.

And cats die. They lie on the floor and lash their tails,
And their reticent fur is suddenly all in motion
With fleas that one never knew were there,
Polished and brown, knowing all there is to know,
Trekking off into the living world.
You fetch a shoe-box, but it's much too small, because
    she won't curl up now:
So you find a bigger box, and bury her in the yard, and
    weep.

But you do not wake up a month from then, two months,
A year from then, two years, in the middle of the night
And weep, with your knuckles in your mouth, and say
    Oh, God! Oh, God!
Childhood is the kingdom where nobody dies that
    matters,—mothers and fathers don't die.

And if you have said, "For heaven's sake, must you
    always be kissing a person?"
Or, "I do wish to gracious you'd stop tapping on the
    window with your thimble!"
Tomorrow, or even the day after tomorrow if you're
    busy having fun,
Is plenty of time to say, "I'm sorry, mother."

To be grown up is to sit at the table with people who
        have died, who neither listen nor speak;
Who do not drink their tea, though they always said
Tea was such a comfort.

Run down into the cellar and bring up the last jar of
        raspberries; they are not tempted.
Flatter them, ask them what was it they said exactly
That time, to the bishop, or to the overseer, or to Mrs.
        Mason;
They are not taken in.
Shout at them, get red in the face, rise,
Drag them up out of their chairs by their stiff shoulders
        and shake them and yell at them;
They are not startled, they are not even embarrassed;
        they slide back into their chairs.

Your tea is cold now.
You drink it standing up,
And leave the house.

The Solid Sprite Who Stands Alone

The solid sprite who stands alone,
    And walks the world with equal stride,
Grieve though he may, is not undone
    Because a friend has died.

He knows that man is born to care,
    And ten and threescore's all his span;
And this is comfort and to spare
    For such a level man.

He is not made like crooked me,
    Who cannot rise nor lift my head,
And all because what had to be
    Has been, what lived is dead;

Who lie among my tears and rust,
    And all because a mortal brain
That loved to think, is clogged with dust,
    And will not think again.

Spring in the Garden

Ah, cannot the curled shoots of the larkspur that you
        loved so,
Cannot the spiny poppy that no winter kills
Instruct you how to return through the thawing ground
        and the thin snow
Into this April sun that is driving the mist between the
        hills?

A good friend to the monkshood in a time of need
You were, and the lupine's friend as well;
But I see the lupine lift the ground like a tough weed
And the earth over the monkshood swell,

And I fear that not a root in all this heaving sea
Of land, has nudged you where you lie, has found
Patience and time to direct you, numb and stupid as you
    still must be
From your first winter underground.

Sonnet

Time, that renews the tissues of this frame,
That built the child and hardened the soft bone,
Taught him to wail, to blink, to walk alone,
Stare, question, wonder, give the world a name,
Forget the watery darkness whence he came,
Attends no less the boy to manhood grown,
Brings him new raiment, strips him of his own:
All skins are shed at length, remorse, even shame.
Such hope is mine, if this indeed be true,
I dread no more the first white in my hair,
Or even age itself, the easy shoe,
The cane, the wrinkled hands, the special chair:
Time, doing this to me, may alter too
My anguish, into something I can bear.

Desolation Dreamed Of

Desolation dreamed of, though not accomplished,
Set my heart to rocking like a boat in a swell.
To every face I met, I said farewell.

Green rollers breaking white along a clean beach . . . when
    shall I reach that island?
Gladly, O painted nails and shaven arm-pits, would I see less
    of you!
Gladly, gladly would I be far from you for a long time, O
    noise and stench of man!

I said farewell. Nevertheless,
Whom have I quitted?—which of my possessions do I
    propose to leave?
Not one. This feigning to be asleep when wide awake is
    all the loneliness
I shall ever achieve.

On the Wide Heath

On the wide heath at evening overtaken,
    When the fast-reddening sun
Drops, and against the sky the looming bracken
    Waves, and the day is done,

Though no unfriendly nostril snuffs his bone,
    Though English wolves be dead,
The fox abroad on errands of his own,
    The adder gone to bed,

The weary traveler from his aching hip
    Lengthens his long stride;
Though Home be but a humming on his lip,
    No happiness, no pride,

He does not drop him under the yellow whin
    To sleep the darkness through;
Home to the yellow light that shines within
    The kitchen of a loud shrew,

Home over stones and sand, through stagnant water
    He goes, mile after mile
Home to a wordless poaching son and a daughter
    With a disdainful smile,

Home to the worn reproach, the disagreeing,
    The shelter, the stale air; content to be
Pecked at, confined, encroached upon,—it being
    Too lonely, to be free.

Two Sonnets in Memory

(Nicola Sacco—Bartolomeo Vanzetti)
Executed August 23, 1927

I

As men have loved their lovers in times past
And sung their wit, their virtue and their grace,
So have we loved sweet Justice to the last,
Who now lies here in an unseemly place.
The child will quit the cradle and grow wise
And stare on beauty till his senses drown;
Yet shall be seen no more by mortal eyes
Such beauty as here walked and here went down.
Like birds that hear the winter crying plain
Her courtiers leave to seek the clement south;
Many have praised her, we alone remain

To break a fist against the lying mouth
Of any man who says this was not so:
Though she be dead now, as indeed we know.

II

Where can the heart be hidden in the ground
And be at peace, and be at peace forever,
Under the world, untroubled by the sound
Of mortal tears, that cease from pouring never?
Well for the heart, by stern compassion harried,
If death be deeper than the churchmen say,—
Gone from this world indeed what's graveward carried,
And laid to rest indeed what's laid away.
Anguish enough while yet the indignant breather
Have blood to spurt upon the oppressor's hand;
Who would eternal be, and hang in ether
A stuffless ghost above his struggling land,
Retching in vain to render up the groan
That is not there, being aching dust's alone?

Conscientious Objector

I shall die, but that is all that I shall do for Death.

I hear him leading his horse out of the stall; I hear the
     clatter on the barn-floor.
He is in haste; he has business in Cuba, business in the
     Balkans, many calls to make this morning.
But I will not hold the bridle while he cinches the girth.
And he may mount by himself: I will not give him a
     leg up.

Though he flick my shoulders with his whip, I will not
     tell him which way the fox ran.
With his hoof on my breast, I will not tell him where
     the black boy hides in the swamp.
I shall die, but that is all that I shall do for Death; I am
     not on his pay-roll.

I will not tell him the whereabouts of my friends nor of
     my enemies either.
Though he promise me much, I will not map him the
     route to any man's door.

Am I a spy in the land of the living, that I should deliver
     men to Death?
Brother, the password and the plans of our city are safe
     with me; never through me
Shall you be overcome.

Epitaph for the Race of Man

I

Before this cooling planet shall be cold,
Long, long before the music of the Lyre,
Like the faint roar of distant breakers rolled
On reefs unseen, when wind and flood conspire
To drive the ship inshore—long, long, I say,
Before this ominous humming hits the ear,
Earth will have come upon a stiller day,
Man and his engines be no longer here.
High on his naked rock the mountain sheep

Will stand alone against the final sky,
Drinking a wind of danger new and deep,
Staring on Vega with a piercing eye,
And gather up his slender hooves and leap
From crag to crag down Chaos, and so go by.

II

When Death was young and bleaching bones were few,
A moving hill against the risen day
The dinosaur at morning made his way,
And dropped his dung upon the blazing dew;
Trees with no name that now are agate grew
Lushly beside him in the steamy clay;
He woke and hungered, rose and stalked his prey,
And slept contented, in a world he knew.
In punctual season, with the race in mind,
His consort held aside her heavy tail,
And took the seed; and heard the seed confined
Roar in her womb; and made a nest to hold
A hatched-out conqueror . . . but to no avail:
The veined and fertile eggs are long since cold.

III

Cretaceous bird, your giant claw no lime
From bark of holly bruised or mistletoe
Could have arrested, could have held you so
Through fifty million years of jostling time;
Yet cradled with you in the catholic slime
Of the young ocean's tepid lapse and flow
Slumbered an agent, weak in embryo,
Should grip you straitly, in its sinewy prime.

What bright collision in the zodiac brews,
What mischief dimples at the planet's core
For shark, for python, for the dove that coos
Under the leaves?—what frosty fate's in store
For the warm blood of man,—man, out of ooze
But lately crawled, and climbing up the shore?

IV

O Earth, unhappy planet born to die,
Might I your scribe and your confessor be,
What wonders must you not relate to me
Of Man, who when his destiny was high
Strode like the sun into the middle sky
And shone an hour, and who so bright as he,
And like the sun went down into the sea,
Leaving no spark to be remembered by.
But no; you have not learned in all these years
To tell the leopard and the newt apart;
Man, with his singular laughter, his droll tears,
His engines and his conscience and his art,
Made but a simple sound upon your ears:
The patient beating of the animal heart.

V

When Man is gone and only gods remain
To stride the world, their mighty bodies hung
With golden shields, and golden curls outflung
Above their childish foreheads; when the plain
Round skull of Man is lifted and again
Abandoned by the ebbing wave, among
The sand and pebbles of the beach,—what tongue

Will tell the marvel of the human brain?
Heavy with music once this windy shell,
Heavy with knowledge of the clustered stars;
The one-time tenant of this draughty hall
Himself, in learned pamphlet, did foretell,
After some aeons of study jarred by wars,
This toothy gourd, this head emptied of all.

VI

See where Capella with her golden kids
Grazes the slope between the east and north:
Thus when the builders of the pyramids
Flung down their tools at nightfall and poured forth
Homeward to supper and a poor man's bed,
Shortening the road with friendly jest and slur,
The risen She-Goat showing blue and red
Climbed the clear dusk, and three stars followed her.
Safe in their linen and their spices lie
The kings of Egypt; even as long ago
Under these constellations, with long eye
And scented limbs they slept, and feared no foe.
Their will was law; their will was not to die:
And so they had their way; or nearly so.

VII

He heard the coughing tiger in the night
Push at his door; close by his quiet head
About the wattled cabin the soft tread
Of heavy feet he followed, and the slight
Sigh of the long banana leaves; in sight
At last and leaning westward overhead

The Centaur and the Cross now heralded
The sun, far off but marching, bringing light.
What time the Centaur and the Cross were spent,
Night and the beast retired into the hill,
Whereat serene and undevoured he lay,
And dozed and stretched and listened and lay still,
Breathing into his body with content
The temperate dawn before the tropic day.

VIII

Observe how Miyanoshita cracked in two
And slid into the valley; he that stood
Grinning with terror in the bamboo wood
Saw the earth heave and thrust its bowels through
The hill, and his own kitchen slide from view,
Spilling the warm bowl of his humble food
Into the lap of horror; mark how lewd
This cluttered gulf,—'twas here his paddy grew.
Dread and dismay have not encompassed him;
The calm sun sets; unhurried and aloof
Into the riven village falls the rain;
Days pass; the ashes cool; he builds again
His paper house upon oblivion's brim,
And plants the purple iris in its roof.

IX

He woke in terror to a sky more bright
Than middle day; he heard the sick earth groan,
And ran to see the lazy-smoking cone
Of the fire-mountain, friendly to his sight
As his wife's hand, gone strange and full of fright;

Over his fleeing shoulder it was shown
Rolling its pitchy lake of scalding stone
Upon his house that had no feet for flight.
Where did he weep? Where did he sit him down
And sorrow, with his head between his knees?
Where said the Race of Man, "Here let me drown"?
"Here let me die of hunger"?—"let me freeze"?
By nightfall he has built another town:
This boiling pot, this clearing in the trees.

X

The broken dike, the levee washed away,
The good fields flooded and the cattle drowned,
Estranged and treacherous all the faithful ground,
And nothing left but floating disarray
Of tree and home uprooted,—was this the day
Man dropped upon his shadow without a sound
And died, having laboured well and having found
His burden heavier than a quilt of clay?
No, no. I saw him when the sun had set
In water, leaning on his single oar
Above his garden faintly glimmering yet . . .
There bulked the plough, here washed the updrifted
    weeds . . .
And scull across his roof and make for shore,
With twisted face and pocket full of seeds.

XI

Sweeter was loss than silver coins to spend,
Sweeter was famine than the belly filled;
Better than blood in the vein was the blood spilled;

Better than corn and healthy flocks to tend
And a tight roof and acres without end
Was the barn burned and the mild creatures killed,
And the back aging fast, and all to build:
For then it was, his neighbour was his friend.
Then for a moment the averted eye
Was turned upon him with benignant beam,
Defiance faltered, and derision slept;
He saw as in a not unhappy dream
The kindly heads against the horrid sky,
And scowled, and cleared his throat and spat, and wept.

XII

Now forth to meadow as the farmer goes
With shining buckets to the milking-ground,
He meets the black ant hurrying from his mound
To milk the aphis pastured on the rose;
But no good-morrow, as you might suppose,
No nod of greeting, no perfunctory sound
Passes between them; no occasion's found
For gossip as to how the fodder grows.
In chilly autumn on the hardening road
They meet again, driving their flocks to stall,
Two herdsmen, each with winter for a goad;
They meet and pass, and never a word at all
Gives one to t'other. On the quaint abode
Of each, the evening and the first snow fall.

XIII

His heatless room the watcher of the stars
Nightly inhabits when the night is clear;
Propping his mattress on the turning sphere,

Saturn his rings or Jupiter his bars
He follows, or the fleeing moons of Mars,
Till from his ticking lens they disappear . . .
Whereat he sighs, and yawns, and on his ear
The busy chirp of Earth remotely jars.
Peace at the void's heart through the wordless night,
A lamb cropping the awful grasses, grazed;
Earthward the trouble lies, where strikes his light
At dawn industrious Man, and unamazed
Goes forth to plough, flinging a ribald stone
At all endeavour alien to his own.

XIV

Him not the golden fang of furious heaven,
Nor whirling Aeolus on his awful wheel,
Nor foggy specter ramming the swift keel,
Nor flood, nor earthquake, nor the red tongue even
Of fire, disaster's dog—him, him bereaven
Of all save the heart's knocking, and to feel
The air upon his face: not the great heel
Of headless Force into the dust has driven.
These sunken cities, tier on tier, bespeak
How ever from the ashes with proud beak
And shining feathers did the phoenix rise,
And sail, and send the vulture from the skies . . .
That in the end returned; for Man was weak
Before the unkindness in his brother's eyes.

XV

Now sets his foot upon the eastern sill
Aldebaran, swiftly rising, mounting high,
And tracks the Pleiads down the crowded sky,

And drives his wedge into the western hill;
Now for the void sets forth, and further still,
The questioning mind of Man . . . that by and by
From the void's rim returns with swooning eye,
Having seen himself into the maelstrom spill.
O race of Adam, blench not lest you find
In the sun's bubbling bowl anonymous death,
Or lost in whistling space without a mind
To monstrous Nothing yield your little breath:
You shall achieve destruction where you stand,
In intimate conflict, at your brother's hand.

XVI

Alas for Man, so stealthily betrayed,
Bearing the bad cell in him from the start,
Pumping and feeding from his healthy heart
That wild disorder never to be stayed
When once established, destined to invade
With angry hordes the true and proper part,
Till Reason joggles in the headsman's cart,
And Mania spits from every balustrade.
Would he had searched his closet for his bane,
Where lurked the trusted ancient of his soul,
Obsequious Greed, and seen that visage plain;
Would he had whittled treason from his side
In his stout youth and bled his body whole,
Then had he died a king, or never died.

XVII

Only the diamond and the diamond's dust
Can render up the diamond unto Man;

One and invulnerable as it began
Had it endured, but for the treacherous thrust
That laid its hard heart open, as it must,
And ground it down and fitted it to span
A turbaned brow or fret an ivory fan,
Lopped of its stature, pared of its proper crust.
So Man, by all the wheels of heaven unscored,
Man, the stout ego, the exuberant mind
No edge could cleave, no acid could consume,—
Being split along the vein by his own kind,
Gives over, rolls upon the palm abhorred,
Is set in brass on the swart thumb of Doom.

XVIII

Here lies, and none to mourn him but the sea,
That falls incessant on the empty shore,
Most various Man, cut down to spring no more;
Before his prime, even in his infancy
Cut down, and all the clamour that was he,
Silenced; and all the riveted pride he wore,
A rusted iron column whose tall core
The rains have tunnelled like an aspen tree.
Man, doughty Man, what power has brought you low,
That heaven itself in arms could not persuade
To lay aside the lever and the spade
And be as dust among the dusts that blow?
Whence, whence the broadside? whose the heavy
        blade? . . .
Strive not to speak, poor scattered mouth; I know.

ANSELMO

Thus are our altars polluted; nor may we flee. The walls
     are strong.
Such erudition as we have we must instantly turn
To practical account; we shall never again have time to
     learn.
For the barbarian has conquered—and our captors
     require of us a song.

Greek may not drown among the islands; it goes down,
But is caught in a net by trawlers, and set
To deciphering postcards from a modern Aegean town.
Nor may wounded Latin lie
Forgotten among the gutter-weeds and die:
It must limp in the Triumph; the lewd and snobbish
     time has use for those proud brows;
Thus Plato survives in a winked-at adjective; and Vergil
Is a name in the advertisement of a cultured dress-
     making house.

RICARDO

It might, of course, be remarked, that the wound in the
     Latin tongue

Was inflicted early, when the Christian Church was
  young . . .
And whether it be preferable that the language of
  Propertius be put to work
As Altar-Boy to an alien faith, or as the clerk
Of a more temporal dominion,
While it may be to the devout a matter of knowledge, is
  to the layman
A matter of opinion.

CARL
(*to Anselmo*)
If your interest in learning is authentic, why not let
  these fellows speak
Each in his own language,—David in Hebrew, Jesus
  in Aramaic; why not read the Epistles in the Greek?
Not at all, you're interested in the spell-binding power
  of a corrupt, a *lingua-franca* Latin chanted
In a burr so thick that if you were imploring Jupiter
  instead of Jesus, he wouldn't know what the hell
  you wanted!

MERTON
(*to Anselmo*)
Anselmo, if I wished to sin and thoroughly enjoy it,
I should join your Church.

Alas, I fear that since I was a child, and dreaded my
  father's wrath, and received my mother's pardon,
I have never known in its fulness the ecstasy of sin.

The Anglo-Saxon, four-square, Protestant man, not
     only strives
To be upright, but intends to be:
Perfection is not only the mark by which he steers, but
     the port where he means
To drop anchor.
This voluptuous sinning-and-forgiving, this quarrelling-
     and-making-up, is not a northern thing.
Your typical angular Protestant, setting out for Heaven,
Knows he has sinned, and prays that his sins be
     forgiven, not because,
Being man, he is sinful, but because he means to sin no
     more.
And he travels light; the taper and the ciborium are
     heavy; and he proposes to arrive
In Heaven on his own feet.
(An impious attitude, this, to Catholic ears.)

As for me, if I did not think I should some day crunch
The carrot before my nose, I should balk in earnest,
And sample the wayside weeds, from that moment on,
With a gourmet's respect.

   PYGMALION
Unwavering hypocrisy, however, and a high ideal,
Make shift to keep us on the road.

Observe, for instance, the sheepy eyes of the next wolf
You see in a tuxedo, haranguing the lambs in the town-
     hall
Over a pitcher of water and under the Stars-and-Stripes;
He means what he says—why, yes, he does—look here,

"Abraham Lincoln!" that's what he says—doesn't he
    mean it?
"Our glorious country!" "Proud to be an American!"
    "Free
And equal!" "Fought and bled!" "This glorious flag!"

Weak eyes?—hell, no!—them's tears!

Do you think *he* thinks he's nothing but a mouth full of
    teeth?—
A larynx raw with lies and in need of a gargle?
A head full of soup?—A shirt full of sawdust, packed
Tight about a frozen heart?—Hell, no; he thinks
He's a darned fine guy!—and he means every promise
    he makes . . .
Means it as a *promise*, I mean. And that's just what I mean.

RICARDO

Hypocrisy is not to be despised. It is the pimp of
    Empire, but it presupposes
The existence in the community of a spiritual force for
    good, that must be courted and betrayed
Into connivance with evil, before the planned step can
    be made.

The overt act of aggression is more dashing to behold,
No doubt, but is impracticable where an articulate
    minority
Is against such acts. Aggression *there* must be sold
To the people under a softer name, for the opposing few
    speak well, and to speak well is to speak with
    authority.

The tyrant is less picturesque than in the old
Days; the high church-going hat crushes somewhat the
    wreath of roses.

Virtue, however, duped and tupped a thousand times by
    Wrong, remains the same,
Is ever virginal, smooths down her tumbled skirts in
    brooding anger, not in shame.

    MERTON
I should prefer, I think, a little less nobility,
And a trifle more intelligence: if Virtue still
After so many Mickey Finns gulps down with such
    docility
Whatever is put to her lips, why, Virtue is an imbecile.

    PYGMALION
I agree. How can we have an ounce of respect, to say
    nothing of this pound of homage for—
How can we have any patience with—a mushy idealism
    like ours today?
Given an intelligent propaganda there's no limit to the
    number of times a nation of pacifists will go to war.
This milk of human kindness is all *soupe au lait.*

    JOHN
Let the lupine human animal doff his sheepskin and
    come squarely out
For the crown of the planet on his pate, and a bloody
    knout
In his paw, and a crushed people—the things he really
    cares about.

Nobody need lie to us any more, we lie so to ourselves,—
    because we can't bear it
That life should be so crass. The wolf in the bed no
    longer need bother
To fit himself out with a ruffled night-cap—certainly he
    needn't wear it—
No matter what he looks like, we tiptoe in with our
    cakes and cry, "Good-day, Grandmother!"

We believe what we are told, without question; Foul
    tells us, "I am Fair,"
And we believe him. "Don't shoot," says the crow in the
    cornfield; "I'm an albatross."
All that the darkey has to say to clear himself when he's
    surprised in the hen-house and the owner calls,
    "Who's there?"
Is, "Just us chickens, boss!"

ANSELMO
(*to Merton*)
To enter into a state of grace with the avowed purpose
    of more poignantly
Experiencing a lapse from grace, is of course impossible.
Our Lord was the victim, mind you, never the butt
Of the unperceiving world.
Faith will not enter even for a moment's time the disin-
    genuous heart, or be the tool of crafty enterprise.
Believing nothing, believing no longer even in yourself,
    your witticism
Gone sour on your tongue, before the serene and
    implacable beauty of the Mass,

Aware that in the presence of duplicity, because of you,
the drama,
Sacred to the single-hearted all about you in that place,
of the anguish suffered
For the redemption of the world by Jesus Christ their
Lord, was being celebrated, shame
Would rise from your sickened breast into your hot
cheek, and your repentance
Would precede your sin, and become, as like as not
Your initial act of Faith.

Strange, that a man who would not play with fire, will
play with God!
You run grave risk, my friend, of being scorched by
Faith.

———

RICARDO
(*to John*)
The mind thrust out of doors,
And not a bone flung after
To hold between its paws
When night and hunger fall,
Leaves the warm house and all
Its grassy lakes of light,
And the good reek of supper;
And trots into the night.

The rabbits hear him come;
The wild-cat on the limb
Whittles its nails to knives,
And crouches over him.

Before the week is out
He leaps at the apple's throat
That hangs in the cold air;
Battens on bark and root,
That never ate such fare.

He harries the lean hill
In vain for winter vermin;
His blunted nose is still
To rabbit on the wind;
His coddled pads are softer
Than vixen's, and they bleed;
He stalks in bitter need,
With hope and belly thinned,
In vain the winter brook
For weasel turned to ermine.

When once the snow lies deep
He harvests where he can;
He wolfs the huddled sheep;
He drinks with drooling lip
The myriad stench of man.

The Snow Storm

No hawk hangs over in this air:
The urgent snow is everywhere.
The wing adroiter than a sail
Must lean away from such a gale,
Abandoning its straight intent,
Or else expose tough ligament
And tender flesh to what before
Meant dampened feathers, nothing more.

Forceless upon our backs there fall
Infrequent flakes hexagonal,
Devised in many a curious style
To charm our safety for a while,
Where close to earth like mice we go
Under the horizontal snow.

Not So Far as the Forest

I

That chill is in the air
Which the wise know well, and even have learned to
    bear.

This joy, I know,
Will soon be under snow.

The sun sets in a cloud
And is not seen.
Beauty, that spoke aloud,
Addresses now only the remembering ear.
The heart begins here
To feed on what has been.

Night falls fast.
Today is in the past.

Blown from the dark hill hither to my door
Three flakes, then four
Arrive, then many more.

II

Branch by branch
This tree has died. Green only
Is one last bough, moving its leaves in the sun.

What evil ate its root, what blight,
What ugly thing,
Let the mole say, the bird sing;
Or the white worm behind the shedding bark
Tick in the dark.

You and I have only one thing to do:
Saw the trunk through.

III

Distressèd mind, forbear
To tease the hooded Why;
That shape will not reply.

From the warm chair
To the wind's welter
Flee, if storm's your shelter.

But no, you needs must part,
Fling him his release—
On whose ungenerous heart
Alone you are at peace.

IV

Not dead of wounds, not borne
Home to the village on a litter of branches, torn
By splendid claws and the talk all night of the villagers,
But stung to death by gnats
Lies Love.

What swamp I sweated through for all these years
Is at length plain to me.

V

Poor passionate thing,
Even with this clipped wing how well you flew!—
    though not so far as the forest.

Unwounded and unspent, serene but for the eye's bright
    trouble,
Was it the lurching flight, the unequal wind under the
    lopped feathers that brought you down,

To sit in folded colours on the level empty field,
Visible as a ship, paling the yellow stubble?

Rebellious bird, warm body foreign and bright,
Has no one told you?—Hopeless is your flight
Towards the high branches. Here is your home,
Between the barnyard strewn with grain and the forest
    tree.
Though Time refeather the wing,
Ankle slip the ring,
The once-confined thing
Is never again free.

"Fontaine, Je Ne Boirai Pas De Ton Eau!"

I know I might have lived in such a way
As to have suffered only pain:
Loving not man nor dog;
Not money, even; feeling
Toothache perhaps, but never more than an hour away
From skill and novocaine;
Making no contacts, dealing with life through agents,
    drinking one cocktail, betting two dollars, wearing
    raincoats in the rain;
Betrayed at length by no one but the fog
Whispering to the wing of the plane.

"Fountain," I have cried to that unbubbling well, "I will
    not drink of thy water!" Yet I thirst

For a mouthful of—not to swallow, only to rinse my
      mouth in—peace. And while the eyes of the past
      condemn,
The eyes of the present narrow into assignation.
      And . . . worst . . .
The young are so old, they are born with their fingers
      crossed; I shall get no help from them.

The True Encounter

"Wolf!" cried my cunning heart
  At every sheep it spied,
  And roused the countryside.

"Wolf! Wolf!"—and up would start
  Good neighbours, bringing spade
  And pitchfork to my aid.

At length my cry was known:
  Therein lay my release.
I met the wolf alone
  And was devoured in peace.

Czecho-Slovakia

If there were balm in Gilead, I would go
To Gilead for your wounds, unhappy land,
Gather you balsam there, and with this hand,
Made deft by pity, cleanse and bind and sew

And drench with healing, that your strength might grow,
(Though love be outlawed, kindness contraband)
And you, O proud and felled, again might stand;
But where to look for balm, I do not know.
The oils and herbs of mercy are so few;
Honour's for sale; allegiance has its price;
The barking of a fox has bought us all;
We save our skins a craven hour or two.—
While Peter warms him in the servants' hall
The thorns are platted and the cock crows twice.

Underground System

Set the foot down with distrust upon the crust of the
        world—it is thin.
Moles are at work beneath us; they have tunnelled the
        sub-soil
With separate chambers, which at an appointed knock
Could be as one, could intersect and interlock. We walk
        on the skin
Of life. No toil
Of rake or hoe, no lime, no phosphate, no rotation of
        crops, no irrigation of the land,
Will coax the limp and flattened grain to stand
On that bad day, or feed to strength the nibbled roots of
        our nation.

Ease has demoralized us, nearly so; we know
Nothing of the rigours of winter: the house has a roof
        against—the car a top against—the snow.

All will be well, we say; it is a habit, like the rising of
    the sun,
For our country to prosper; who can prevail against us?
    No one.
The house has a roof; but the boards of its floor are
    rotting, and hall upon hall
The moles have built their palace beneath us: we have
    not far to fall.

Two Voices

FIRST VOICE

Let us be circumspect, surrounded as we are
By every foe but one, and he from the woods watching.
Let us be courteous, since we cannot be wise, guilty of
    no neglect, pallid with seemly terror, yet regarding
    with indulgent eyes
Violence, and compromise.

SECOND VOICE

We shall learn nothing; or we shall learn it too late.
    Why should we wait
For Death, who knows the road so well? Need we sit
    hatching—
Such quiet fowl as we, meek to the touch,—a clutch of
    adder's eggs? Let us not turn them; let us not keep
    them warm; let us leave our nests and flock and tell
All that we know, all that we can piece together, of a
    time when all went, or seemed to go, well.

This Dusky Faith

Why, then, weep not,
Since naught's to weep.

Too wild, too hot
For a dead thing,
Altered and cold,
Are these long tears:
Relinquishing
To the sovereign force
Of the pulling past
What you cannot hold
Is reason's course.

Wherefore, sleep.

Or sleep to the rocking
Rather, of this:
The silver knocking
Of the moon's knuckles
At the door of the night;
Death here becomes
Being, nor truckles
To the sun, assumes
Light as its right.

So, too, this dusky faith
In Man, transcends its death,
Shines out, gains emphasis;
Shorn of the tangled past,
Shows its fine skull at last,
Cold, lovely satellite.

To a Young Poet

Time cannot break the bird's wing from the bird.
Bird and wing together
Go down, one feather.

No thing that ever flew,
Not the lark, not you,
Can die as others do.

To Elinor Wylie

(*Died 1928*)

I
Song for a Lute
(*1927*)

Seeing how I love you utterly,
And your disdain is my despair,
Alter this dulcet eye, forbear
To wear those looks that latterly
You wore, and won me wholly, wear
A brow more dark, and bitterly
Berate my dulness and my care,
Seeing how your smile is my despair,
Seeing how I love you utterly.

Seeing how I love you utterly,
And your distress is my despair,
Alter this brimming eye, nor wear

The trembling lip that latterly
Under a more auspicious air
You wore, and thrust me through, forbear
To drop your head so bitterly
Into your hands, seeing how I dare
No tender touch upon your hair,
Knowing as I do how fitterly
You do reproach me than forbear,
Seeing how your tears are my despair,
Seeing how I love you utterly.

II
(*1928*)

For you there is no song . . .
    Only the shaking
Of the voice that meant to sing; the sound of the strong
    Voice breaking.

Strange in my hand appears
    The pen, and yours broken.
There are ink and tears on the page; only the tears
    Have spoken.

III
Sonnet in Answer to a Question
(*1938*)

Oh, she was beautiful in every part!—
The auburn hair that bound the subtle brain;
The lovely mouth cut clear by wit and pain,

Uttering oaths and nonsense, uttering art
In casual speech and curving at the smart
On startled ears of excellence too plain
For early morning!—*Obit.* Death from strain;
The soaring mind outstripped the tethered heart.

Yet here was one who had no need to die
To be remembered. Every word she said
The lively malice of the hazel eye
Scanning the thumb-nail close—oh, dazzling dead,
How like a comet through the darkening sky
You raced! . . . would your return were heralded.

IV

Nobody now throughout the pleasant day,
The flowers well tended and the friends not few,
Teases my mind as only you could do
To mortal combat erudite and gay . . .
"So Mr. S. was kind to Mr. K.!
Whilst Mr. K.—wait, I've a word or two!"
(I think that Keats and Shelley died with you—
They live on paper now, another way.)

You left in time, too soon; to leave too soon
Was tragic and in order—had the great
Not taught us how to die?—My simple blood,
Loving you early, lives to mourn you late . . .
As Mr. K., it may be, would have done;
As Mr. S. (*oh, answer!*) never would.

V

Gone over to the enemy now and marshalled against me
Is my best friend.
What hope have I to hold with my narrow back
This town, whence all surrender?

Someone within these walls has been in love with Death
        longer than I care to say;
It was not you! . . . but he gets in that way.

Gone under cover of darkness, leaving a running track,
And the mark of a dusty paw on all our splendour,
Are they that smote the table with the loudest blow,
Saying, "I will not have it so!"

No, no.
This is the end.
What hope have I?
You, too, led captive and without a cry!

VI

Over the Hollow Land

Over the hollow land the nightingale
Sang out in the full moonlight.
"Immortal bird,"
We said, who heard;
"What rapture, what serene despair";
And paused between a question and reply
To hear his varied song across the tulip-scented air.

But I thought of the small brown bird among the
  rhododendrons at the garden's end,
Crouching, close to the bough,
Pale cheek wherefrom the black magnificent eye
  obliquely stared,
The great song boiling in the narrow throat
And the beak near splitting,
A small bird hunched and frail,
Whom the divine uncompromising note that brought
  the world to its window
Shook from head to tail.
Close to the branch, I thought, he cowers now,
Lest his own passion shake him from the bough.

Thinking of him, I thought of you . . .
Shaken from the bough, and the pure song half-way
  through.

——

Now that the west is washed of clouds and clear,
The sun gone under and his beams laid by,
You, that require a quarter of the sky
To shine alone in: prick the dusk, appear,
Beautiful Venus! The dense atmosphere
Cannot diffuse your rays, you blaze so high,
Lighting with loveliness a crisp and dry
Cold evening in the autumn of the year.
The pilot standing by his broken plane

In the unheard-of mountains, looks on you,
And warms his heart a moment at your light . . .
Benignant planet, sweet, familiar sight . . .
Thinking he may be found, he may again
See home, breaks the stale buttered crust in two.

———

I too beneath your moon, almighty Sex,
Go forth at nightfall crying like a cat,
Leaving the lofty tower I laboured at
For birds to foul and boys and girls to vex
With tittering chalk; and you, and the long necks
Of neighbours sitting where their mothers sat
Are well aware of shadowy this and that
In me, that's neither noble nor complex.
Such as I am, however, I have brought
To what it is, this tower; it is my own;
Though it was reared To Beauty, it was wrought
From what I had to build with: honest bone
Is there, and anguish; pride; and burning thought;
And lust is there, and nights not spent alone.

———

Thou famished grave, I will not fill thee yet,
Roar though thou dost, I am too happy here;
Gnaw thine own sides, fast on; I have no fear

Of thy dark project, but my heart is set
On living—I have heroes to beget
Before I die; I will not come anear
Thy dismal jaws for many a splendid year;
Till I be old, I aim not to be eat.
I cannot starve thee out: I am thy prey
And thou shalt have me; but I dare defend
That I can stave thee off; and I dare say,
What with the life I lead, the force I spend,
I'll be but bones and jewels on that day,
And leave thee hungry even in the end.

———

Not only love plus awful grief,
The ardent and consuming pain
Of all who loved and who remain
To tend alone the buried brief
Eternal, propping laurel-leaf
And frozen rose above the slain,—
But pity lest they die again
Makes of the mind an iron sheaf
Of bundled memories. Ah, bright ghost,
Who shadow all I have and do,
Be gracious in your turn, be gone!
Suffice it that I loved you most.
I would be rid of even you,
And see the world I look upon.

Make bright the arrows,
    Gather the shields:
Conquest narrows
    The peaceful fields.

Stock well the quiver
    With arrows bright:
The bowman feared
    Need never fight.

Make bright the arrows,
    O peaceful and wise!
Gather the shields
    Against surprise.

An Eclipse of the Sun Is Predicted

I never was one to go to war against the weather, against
        the bad conditions
Prevailing, though prevailing for a long time, the sullen
        spring,
The ugly summer grey and cold;
"Summer will bud"; I said; "Autumn do the blossoming;
Winter curtail a year without fruitions;
I, starving a little, await the new bounty as of old."

I have gone to war, I am at war, I am at grips
With that which threatens more than a cold summer;
I am at war with the shadow, at war with the sun's
    eclipse,
Total, and not for a minute, but for all my days.
Under that established twilight how could I raise
Beans and corn? I am at war with the black newcomer.

"Gentlemen Cry, Peace!"

There is no Peace; had we again the choice
Whether to build our sinews to such force
None dare affront us, or to seek divorce
From the blunt, factual time, and with soft voice
Blandish the past to give us back our toys
Faded but still so dear,—we should of course
Forego tranquillity without remorse,
Gird us for battle . . . and in peace rejoice.

But now . . . what power to bargain have the poor?
And, in those iron values which alone
Pass in our time for legal currency,
Minted by savage chieftains to insure
Shut mouth, shut mind, hushed sobbing, swallowed
    groan
And punished laughter—who so poor as we?

———

I must not die of pity; I must live;
Grow strong, not sicken; eat, digest my food,
That it may build me, and in doing good
To blood and bone, broaden the sensitive
Fastidious pale perception: we contrive
Lean comfort for the starving, who intrude
Upon them with our pots of pity; brewed
From stronger meat must be the broth we give.
Blue, bright September day, with here and there
On the green hills a maple turning red,
And white clouds racing in the windy air!—
If I would help the weak, I must be fed
In wit and purpose, pour away despair
And rinse the cup, eat happiness like bread.

THE MURDER OF LIDICE | 1942

They marched them out to the public square,
Two hundred men in a row;
And every step of the distance there,
Each stone in the road, each man did know,
And every alley and doorway where
As a carefree boy, not long ago,
With boys of his age he would hide and run
And shout, in the days when everyone
Was safe, and free, and school was out . . .
Not very long ago . . .
And he felt on his face the soft June air,
And thought, "This cannot be so!"

The friendly houses, the little inn
Where times without number he had been
Of an evening, and talked with his neighbors there
Of planting and politics (not a chair
At any table he had not sat in)
And welcomed the newcomer coming in
With nod of greeting, or "Look who's here!"—
Spoken friendly across the rim
Of a mug of Pilsen beer.

And the men he had greeted with loving shout,
And talked about football with, and about

The crops, and how to keep Hitler out . . .
Were lined up with him here.

And one man thought of the sunny row
In his garden, where he had left his hoe;
And one man thought of the walnut trees
He had climbed, and the day he broke his arm . . .
But it had not hurt, as his mind hurt now . . .
How happy his boyhood, how free from harm!
And one, who was dying, opened his eyes,
For he smelled smoke, and stared at the skies
Cloudy and lurid with smoke and flame;
From every building it billowed; it came
From every roof, and out it burst
At every window—none was the first;
From every window about him burst
The terrible shape of flame,
And clawed at the sky, and leapt to the ground,
And ran through the village with a crackling sound
And a sudden roar where a roof fell in;
And he thought of his mother, left alone
In the house, not able to rise from her chair;
And he got to his elbows, and tried to crawl
To his home, across the blood in the square,
But at every step did slip and fall,
For the slippery blood was everywhere.

Oh, many a faithful dog that day
Stood by his master's body at bay,
And tugged at the sleeve of an arm outflung;
Or laid his paws on his master's breast,

With panting jaws and whimpering cries,
Gazing into his glazing eyes
And licking his face with loving tongue;
Nor would from his master's body depart,
Till they kicked in his ribs and crushed his heart.

Small Hands, Relinquish All

Small hands, relinquish all:
Nothing the fist can hold,—
Not power, not love, not gold—
But suffers from the cold,
And is about to fall.

The mind, at length bereft
Of thinking, and its pain,
Will soon disperse again,
And nothing will remain:
No, not a thought be left.

Exhort the closing eye,
Urge the resisting ear,
To say, "The thrush is here";
To say, "His song is clear";
To live, before it die.

Small hands, relinquish all:
Nothing the fist can hold,
Not power, not love, not gold,
But suffers from the cold,
And is about to fall.

The mind, at length bereft
Of thinking and its pain,
Will soon disperse again,
And nothing will remain:
No, not a thing be left.

Only the ardent eye,
Only the listening ear
Can say, "The thrush was here!"
Can say, "His song was clear!"
Can live, before it die.

Ragged Island

There, there where those black spruces crowd
To the edge of the precipitous cliff,
Above your boat, under the eastern wall of the island;
And no wave breaks; as if
All had been done, and long ago, that needed
Doing; and the cold tide, unimpeded
By shoal or shelving ledge, moves up and down,
Instead of in and out;
And there is no driftwood there, because there is no
     beach;
Clean cliff going down as deep as clear water can reach;

No driftwood, such as abounds on the roaring shingle,
To be hefted home, for fires in the kitchen stove;
Barrels, banged ashore about the boiling outer harbour;
Lobster-buoys, on the eel-grass of the sheltered cove:

There, thought unbraids itself, and the mind becomes
    single.
There you row with tranquil oars, and the ocean
Shows no scar from the cutting of your placid keel;
Care becomes senseless there; pride and promotion
Remote; you only look; you scarcely feel.

Even adventure, with its vital uses,
Is aimless ardour now; and thrift is waste.

Oh, to be there, under the silent spruces,
Where the wide, quiet evening darkens without haste
Over a sea with death acquainted, yet forever chaste.

——

To whom the house of Montagu
Was neighbour, and that orchard near
Wherein all pleasant fruit-trees grew
Whose tops were silvered by the clear
Light of the blessèd, sworn-by moon,
(Or all-but-sworn-by—save that She,
Knowing the moon's inconstancy,
Dreaded that Love might change as soon . . .
Which changèd never; or did change
Into something rich and strange);
To whom in infancy the sight
Of Sancho Panza and his Knight,
In noble, sad and awkward state
Approaching through the picket-gate,

Was warmer with the flesh of life
Than visits from the vicar's wife;
For whom from earliest days the lips
Of Her who launched the thousand ships
Curved in entrancing speech, and Troy
Was hurt by no historic boy,
But one more close and less a fool
Than boys who yanked your curls at school
(Far less a fool than he who lay
With willing Venus on a bed
Of anise, parsley, dill and rue,
A bank whereon the wild thyme grew,
And longed but to be gone from thence,—
Whom vainly Venus did implore
To do her that sweet violence
All boys and girls with any sense
Would die to do; but where she lay
Left her, and rose and rushed away
To stalk the tusky, small-eyed boar
He might have stalked another day),
And naked long Leander swam
The Thames, the Avon and the Cam,
And wet and chattering, white and cold
Appeared upon the pure threshold
Of Hero, whom the sight did move
To fear, to pity, and to love;

For such a child the peopled time,
When any man in any wood
Was shaggy like a goat, and stood
On hooves, and used his lusty strength
To blow through straws of different length

Bound all together; or could ride
A horse he never need bestride—
For such a child, that distant time
Was close as apple-trees to climb,
And apples crashed among the trees
Half Baldwin, half Hesperides.

——

The courage that my mother had
Went with her, and is with her still:
Rock from New England quarried;
Now granite in a granite hill.

The golden brooch my mother wore
She left behind for me to wear;
I have no thing I treasure more:
Yet, it is something I could spare.

Oh, if instead she'd left to me
The thing she took into the grave!—
That courage like a rock, which she
Has no more need of, and I have.

Armenonville

By the lake at Armenonville in the Bois de Boulogne
Small begonias had been set in the embankment, both
    pink and red;
With polished leaf and brittle, juicy stem;

They covered the embankment; there were wagon-loads
    of them,
Charming and neat, gay colours in the warm shade.

We had preferred a table near the lake, half out of view,
Well out of hearing, for a voice not raised above
A low, impassioned question and its low reply.
We both leaned forward with our elbows on the table,
    and you
Watched my mouth while I answered, and it made me
    shy.
I looked about, but the waiters knew we were in love,
And matter-of-factly left us blissfully alone.

There swam across the lake, as I looked aside, avoiding
Your eyes for a moment, there swam from under the
    pink and red begonias
A small creature; I thought it was a water-rat; it swam
    very well,
In complete silence, and making no ripples at all
Hardly; and when suddenly I turned again to you,
Aware that you were speaking, and perhaps had been
    speaking for some time,
I was aghast at my absence, for truly I did not know
Whether you had been asking or telling.

Dream of Saba

Calm was Half-Moon Bay; we lay at anchor there
Just off Tortola; when the hurricane,

Leaving its charted path, leapt full upon us,
And we were bruised and sobbing from the blows of the
  rain
Before we knew by what we were attacked or could in
  any way prepare.

"How dark it is tonight!" someone had said.
The lantern in the rigging burned serene
Through its glass chimney without crack and polished
  clean;
The wick well trimmed; plenty of kerosene.
We went to bed.

Following a fearful night I do not quite remember came
  a kind of dawn, not light,
But something we could see by. And we saw
What we had missed by inches: what we were headed
  for.

Astern, in an empty sea,
Suddenly, and before a man could cry, "Look there!"
Appeared what for an instant seemed to be
Black backs of half a hundred porpoises.
Before the eyes could blink at these,
They were black reefs, which rose into the air
With awful speed till they were mountains; these, one
  moment there,
Streaming sea-water stood against the sky;
Then all together and with awful speed diminished and
  like porpoises were gone,
Leaving the sea bare.

We turned from staring aft, and dead ahead, a mile
    away,
It seemed, through the thick steam of a white boiling
    surf and through smashed spray,
Saw the tall naked grooved precipitous sides and
    concave top
Of a volcanic island—its volcano now extinct,
It seemed; but it was hard to say.
From its high crater no red flame
Was seen to pulse and pour
But was it indeed or was it alone the steam from
    the burning breakers that kept us from seeing
    more?

There was no harbour. Those steep sides without a
    strand
Went down.
Yet even as from eye to brain this swift perception
    flashed, there seemed to reach
Even more swiftly toward us from that island now
    miraculously in height and size increased
A broadening sandless beach
Humped with round boulders mossed with brightest
    green,
And purple with prostrate sea-ferns and stiff upright
    purple fans;
Red with anemones, and brilliant blue, and yellow
    dotted with black
From many fishes, lashing in the draining pools
Or sliding down the narrow sluices from the
    encroaching land to the receding sea.

The water thinned; we saw beneath us now
The bottom clearly; and from the vessel's bow
Saw close ahead, in shallow pool or dripping crevice
        caught,
The lovely fishes, rosy with azure fins or cobalt blue or
        yellow striped with black,
Curve their bright bodies double and lash forth and leap
        and then fall back with heavy splash
Or from the crevice leap and on the slippery weeds slide
        down once more into the narrow crack.

The thump and scrape of our keel upon the shore
Shook us from horror to a friendly sound!
Danger, maybe death, but decent, and the cause
        known.
Yet neither hook nor oar
Was overside before a Wave like a giant's palm
Was under us and raising us, gently, straight into the
        sky.
We rose beside the cliffs; we passed them so close by
We saw some little plants with reddish-purple flowers
Growing in a rock; and lying on a narrow ledge
Some birds' eggs; and some birds screamed at us as we
        passed.

The Wave did not break against the cliff; with utmost
        calm
It lifted us. The cliff had niches now where green grass
        grew.
And on a foot-high bush in a cleft some raspberries
        were ripe. And then at last

We saw the crater's edge.
The Wave curved over the rim and set us down in a
    cradle of branches, and withdrew.

It has not returned. Far down, the roaring of the sea
    abates
From hour to hour. The sky above our bowl is blue.

For Warmth Alone, for Shelter Only

For warmth alone, for shelter only
From the cold anger of the eyeless wind,
That knows my whereabouts, and mainly
To be at your door when I go down
Is abroad at all tonight in town,
I left my phrase in air, and sinned,
Laying my head against your arm
A moment, and as suddenly
Withdrawing it, and sitting there,
Warmed a little but far from warm,
And the wind still waiting at the foot of the stair,
And much harm done, and the phrase in air.

———

Black hair you'd say she had, or rather
Black crest, black nape and black lore-feather
Above the eye; eye black, and ring
About it white, white breast and wing;

Soft bill; (no predatory thing—
Three claws in front and one in back
But sparrow-fingered, for attack
Unfitted)—yet the questioning,
The desperate notes I did not hear,
Being pitched too high for human ear,
But seen so plainly in the eye
She turned upon me urgently
And watched me with as she went by
And close before me following,
Perching, and ever peering back,
Uttered, I know, some desperate cry,
I might have answered, had I heard:—
Ah, no; ah, no; poor female bird
With unmelodious throat and wing:
Sit on your eggs, by crimson king
Or gold made fertile; hatch them, bring
Beauty to birth, that it may sing
And leave you; be not haggard; cling
To what you have: a coloured thing
That grows more coloured every spring,
And whilst you warm his eggs, no lack
Will let you suffer: when they crack—
Feed them, and feed yourself; whilst he
Hangs from a thistle drunkenly,
Or loops his little flights between
The maple and the evergreen.
Utter your querulous chirp or quack;
And if his voice be anything,
Why, shut your lids and hear him sing,
And when he wants you, take him back.

Steepletop

I

Even you, Sweet Basil: even you,
Lemon Verbena: must exert yourselves now and
    somewhat harden
Against untimely frost; I have hovered you and covered
    you and kept going smudges,
Until I am close to worn-out. Now, you
Go about it. I have other things to do,
Writing poetry, for instance. And I, too,
Live in this garden.

II

Nothing could stand
All this rain.
The lilacs were drowned, browned before I had even
    smelled them
Cool against my cheek, held down
A little by my hand.

Pain
Is seldom preventable, but is presentable
Even to strangers on a train—
But what the rain
Does to the lilacs—is something you must sigh and try
To explain.

III

Borage, forage for bees
And for those who love blue,
Why must you,
Having only been transplanted
From where you were not wanted
Either by the bee or by me
From under the sage, engage in this self-destruction?
I was tender about your slender tap-root.
I thought you would send out shoot after shoot
Of thick cucumber-smelling, hairy leaves.
But why anybody believes
Anything, I do not know. I thought I could trust you.

———

Look how the bittersweet with lazy muscle moves aside
Great stones placed here by planning men not without
    sweat and pride.
And yet how beautiful this broken wall applied
No more to its first duty: to keep sheep or cattle in;
Bought up by Beauty now, with the whole calm
    abandoned countryside.

And how the bittersweet to meet the stunned admiring
    eye with all
The red and orange splendour of its fruit at the first
    stare
Unclasps its covering leaves, lets them all fall,
Strips to the twig, is bare.

See, too, the nightshade, the woody, the bittersweet,
      strangling the wall
For this, the beauty of berries, this scandalous, bright
Persimmon and tangerine comment on fieldstone, on
      granite and on quartz, by might
Of men and crowbars, and a rock for lever, and a rock
      above a rock wedged in, and the leverage right,
Wrested from the tough acres that in time must yield
And suffer plow and harrow and be a man's hay-field—
Wrested, hoisted, balanced on its edge, tipped, tumbled,
      clear
Of its smooth-walled cool hole lying, dark and damp
      side upward in the sun, inched and urged upon the
      stone-boat, hauled here.

Yet mark where the rowan, the mountain ash berries,
      hang bunched amid leaves like ferns,
Scarlet in clear blue air, and the tamarack turns
Yellow as mustard, and sheds its short needles to lie on
      the ground like light
Through the door of a hut in the forest to travellers
      miles off the road at night;
Where brilliant the briony glows in the hedge, frail,
      clustered, elliptical fruit;
Nightshade conserving in capsules transparent of
      jacinth and amber its jellies of ill-repute.

And only the cherries, that ripened for robins and
      cherry-birds, burned
With more ruddy a spark than the bark and the leaves of
      the cherry-tree, red in October turned.

Those hours when happy hours were my estate,—
Entailed, as proper, for the next in line,
Yet mine the harvest, and the title mine—
Those acres, fertile, and the furrow straight,
From which the lark would rise—all of my late
Enchantments, still, in brilliant colours, shine,
But striped with black, the tulip, lawn and vine,
Like gardens looked at through an iron gate.
Yet not as one who never sojourned there
I view the lovely segments of a past
I lived with all my senses, well aware
That this was perfect, and it would not last:
I smell the flower, though vacuum-still the air;
I feel its texture, though the gate is fast.

———

Not, to me, less lavish—though my dreams have been
    splendid—
Than dreams, have been the hours of the actual day:
Never, awaking, did I awake to say:
"Nothing could be like that," when a dream was ended.
Colours, in dream; ecstasy, in dream extended
Beyond the edge of sleep—these, in their way,
Approach, come even close, yet pause, yet stay,
In the high presence of request by its answer attended.

Music, and painting, poetry, love, and grief,
Had they been more intense, I could not have borne,—
Yet, not, I think, through stout endurance lacked;
Rather, because the budding and the falling leaf
Were one, and wonderful,—not to be torn
Apart: I ask of dream: seem like the fact.

———

Tranquility at length, when autumn comes,
Will lie upon the spirit like that haze
Touching far islands on fine autumn days
With tenderest blue, like bloom on purple plums;
Harvest will ring, but not as summer hums,
With noisy enterprise—to broaden, raise,
Proceed, proclaim, establish: autumn stays
The marching year one moment; stills the drums.
Then sits the insistent cricket in the grass;
But on the gravel crawls the chilly bee;
And all is over that could come to pass
Last year; excepting this: the mind is free
One moment, to compute, refute, amass,
Catalogue, question, contemplate, and see.

Sonnet in Dialectic

And is indeed truth beauty?—at the cost
Of all else that we cared for, can this be?—

To see the coarse triumphant, and to see
Honour and pity ridiculed, and tossed
Upon a poked-at fire; all courage lost
Save what is whelped and fattened by decree
To move among the unsuspecting free
And trap the thoughtful, with their thoughts engrossed?
Drag yet that stream for Beauty, if you will;
And find her, if you can; finding her drowned
Will not dismay your ethics,—you will still
To one and all insist she has been found . . .
And haggard men will smile your praise, until,
Some day, they stumble on her burial-mound.

———

It is the fashion now to wave aside
As tedious, obvious, vacuous, trivial, trite,
All things which do not tickle, tease, excite
To some subversion, or in verbiage hide
Intent, or mock, or with hot sauce provide
A dish to prick the thickened appetite;
Straightforwardness is wrong, evasion right;
It is correct, *de rigueur*, to deride.
What fumy wits these modern wags expose,
For all their versatility: Voltaire,
Who wore to bed a night-cap, and would close,
In fear of drafts, all windows, could declare
In antique stuffiness, a phrase that blows
Still through men's smoky minds, and clears the air.

———

Alcestis to her husband, just before, with his tearful approbation,
she dies in order that he may live.

Admetus, from my marrow's core I do
Despise you: wherefore pity not your wife,
Who, having seen expire her love for you
With heaviest grief, today gives up her life.
You could not with your mind imagine this:
One might surrender, yet continue proud.
Not having loved, you do not know: the kiss
You sadly beg, is impious, not allowed.
Of all I loved,—how many girls and men
Have loved me in return?—speak!—young or old—
Speak!—sleek or famished, can you find me then
One form would flank me, as this night grows cold?
I am at peace, Admetus—go and slake
Your grief with wine. I die for my own sake.

———

I will put Chaos into fourteen lines
And keep him there; and let him thence escape
If he be lucky; let him twist, and ape
Flood, fire, and demon—his adroit designs
Will strain to nothing in the strict confines
Of this sweet Order, where, in pious rape,
I hold his essence and amorphous shape,
Till he with Order mingles and combines.

Past are the hours, the years, of our duress,
His arrogance, our awful servitude:
I have him. He is nothing more nor less
Than something simple not yet understood;
I shall not even force him to confess;
Or answer. I will only make him good.

―――

And must I then, indeed, Pain, live with you
All through my life?—sharing my fire, my bed,
Sharing—oh, worst of all things!—the same head?—
And, when I feed myself, feeding you, too?
So be it, then, if what seems true, is true:
Let us to dinner, comrade, and be fed;—
I cannot die till you yourself are dead,
And, with you living, I can live life through.
Yet have you done me harm, ungracious guest,
Spying upon my ardent offices
With frosty look; robbing my nights of rest;
And making harder things I did with ease.
You will die with me: but I shall, at best,
Forgive you with restraint, for deeds like these.

―――

Felicity of Grief!—even Death being kind,
Reminding us how much we dared to love!
There, once, the challenge lay,—like a light glove

Dropped as through carelessness—easy to find
Means and excuse for being somewhat blind
Just at that moment; and why bend above,
Take up, such certain anguish for the mind?
Ah, you who suffer now as I now do,
Seeing, of Life's dimensions, not one left
Save Time—long days somehow to be lived through:
Think—of how great a thing were you bereft
That it should weigh so now!—and that you knew
Always, its awkward contours, and its heft.

_____

If I die solvent—die, that is to say,
In full possession of my critical mind,
Not having cast, to keep the wolves at bay
In this dark wood—till all be flung behind—
Wit, courage, honour, pride, oblivion
Of the red eyeball and the yellow tooth;
Nor sweat nor howl nor break into a run
When loping Death's upon me in hot sooth;
'Twill be that in my honoured hands I bear
What's under no condition to be spilled
Till my blood spills and hardens in the air:
An earthen grail, a humble vessel filled
To its low brim with water from that brink
Where Shakespeare, Keats and Chaucer learned to drink.

BIOGRAPHICAL NOTE

NOTE ON THE TEXTS

NOTES

INDEX OF TITLES &
FIRST LINES

BIOGRAPHICAL NOTE

Edna St. Vincent Millay was born February 22, 1892, in Rockland, Maine. Her parents were divorced in 1900, and her mother took the three children to Camden, Maine, where she worked as a nurse to support the family. Millay submitted "Renascence," a long poem, to a 1912 poetry contest sponsored by the anthology *The Lyric Year*; it came in fourth, but was praised by the poets Witter Bynner and Arthur Davison Ficke, establishing Millay's literary reputation. She entered Vassar College in 1914. After graduating in 1917, she moved to Greenwich Village, and her first book, *Renascence and Other Poems*, was published. She wrote and directed the verse play *Aria da Capo* for the Provincetown Players in 1919. After traveling in Europe from 1921 to 1923, she married Eugen Boissevain, and bought the farm Steepletop in Austerlitz, New York. In 1927 she wrote the libretto for Deems Taylor's opera *The King's Henchman*. She was elected in 1929 to the National Institute of Arts and Letters. With George Dillon, she translated Baudelaire's *Flowers of Evil* (1936). She received the Gold Medal of the Poetry Society of America in 1943. She died on October 19, 1950. Her *Collected Poems* (1956) was edited by her sister Norma Millay Ellis.

NOTE ON THE TEXTS

The texts of the poems in this volume are taken from *Collected Poems* (New York: Harper & Row, 1956), edited by Norma Millay, except for works not included in that edition. The texts of poems that do not appear in *Collected Poems* are printed from the following sources:

Aria da Capo. *Aria da Capo* (New York: Mitchell Kennerley, 1921).
from The King's Henchman: *The King's Henchman* (New York: Harper & Brothers, 1927). The titles of the excerpts were added by the editor of the present volume.
Translations from Flowers of Evil: *Flowers of Evil: From the French of Charles Baudelaire by George Dillon and Edna St. Vincent Millay* (New York: Harper & Brothers, 1936).
from Conversation at Midnight: *Conversation at Midnight* (New York: Harper & Brothers, 1937).
Make Bright the Arrows, An Eclipse of the Sun Is Predicted, "Gentlemen Cry, Peace!": *Make Bright the Arrows: 1940 Notebook* (New York: Harper & Brothers, 1940).
from The Murder of Lidice: *The Murder of Lidice* (New York: Harper & Brothers, 1942).

This volume corrects the following typographical errors in the source texts, cited by page and line numbers: 53.13, vine,;

54.17, burn,; 73.18, without; 96.8, without; 113.5 drowned;; 134.2. words!—

The following is a list of pages where a stanza break coincides with the foot of the page (except where such breaks are apparent from the regular stanzaic structure of the poem): 100, 108, 112, 147, 148, 149, 152, 155, 167, 170, 172, 185, 189, 196, 201, 202, 207.

NOTES

30.1   Passer Mortuus Est]   Catullus III.1: "The sparrow is dead." The reference is to a pet of Catullus's mistress, Lesbia.

68.1   To Inez Milholland]   American feminist and social activist (1886–1916), the first wife of Millay's husband, Eugen Boissevain. This poem was originally entitled "The Pioneer."

68.3   *three leaders*]   Lucretia Mott, Susan B. Anthony, and Elizabeth Cady Stanton.

73.2   *ARIA DA CAPO*]   The 1921 Mitchell Kennerley edition provides the following cast list:

> ORIGINAL CAST
> [As played by the Provincetown Players, New York City]
> PIERROT: HARRISON DOWD
> COLUMBINE: NORMA MILLAY
> COTHURNUS: HUGH FERRISS
> CORYDON: CHARLES ELLIS
> THYRSIS: JAMES LIGHT

105.1–2   TRANSLATIONS FROM *FLOWERS OF EVIL*]   The French titles of the poems (or first lines of untitled poems) translated here are: L'Avertisseur; Rêve parisien; L'Invitation au voyage; "La servante au grand cœur dont vous étiez jalouse"; Spleen (I) ("Pluviôse, irrité contre la ville entière"); Spleen (III) ("Je suis comme le roi d'un pays pluvieux"); Brumes et pluies; "Je n'ai pas oublié, voisine de la ville."

111.2   Pluviose]   January 21 to February 19, according to the new calendar established after the French Revolution.

117.1   *FATAL INTERVIEW*]   Millay dedicated this book to Elinor Wylie; her dedication includes the following lines:

> When I think of you,
> I die, too.
> In my throat, bereft
> Like yours, of air,
> No sound is left,
> Nothing is there
> To make a word of grief.

124.11   the Sparrow-Drawn]   Venus.

124.12   her arrowy child,]   Cupid.

124.21–22   Forsworn Aeneas . . . shore]   Cf. *Aeneid*, Book IV, lines 579–80 (in the Loeb edition).

124.24   The brooch . . . Greek.]   During the Trojan War, Cressida pledged fidelity to her lover Troilus shortly before being offered to the Greeks in exchange for the return of three Trojan princes; she broke her vow soon after the exchange, giving tokens of Troilus's pledge to her Greek lover Diomedes.

125.1–2   Danae . . . golden Jove]   Jove visited Danaë, who had been imprisoned in a tower by her father Acrisius, by transforming himself into a shower of gold. Perseus was born from their union.

125.4   the Swan's featherless bride.]   Jove seduced Leda, the daughter of king of Aetolia, by assuming the form of a swan.

143.2–3   Latmian cave . . . Moon!]   In Greek myth and by poetic tradition, the Moon descended to visit Endymion, a handsome shepherd of Mount Latmos, and chastely admired his beauty as he slept.

160.10   Miyanoshita]   The resort town of Miyanoshita, Japan, lies in the crater of what was once a large volcano.

177.12   "Fontaine . . . Eau!"]   From the French proverb, "Il ne faut jamais dire, 'Fontaine, je ne boirai pas de ton eau!'" ("You should never say, 'Fountain, I'll never drink your water!'")

178.20   If there . . . Gilead,]   Cf. Jeremiah 8:22.

179.9–10   While Peter . . . twice.]   Cf. Mark 14: 67–72.

196.11   Ragged Island]   A small island in Casco Bay off the coast of Maine which Millay and her husband bought in July 1933.

212.1–2   *Alcestis . . . may live.*]   In Euripides' *Alcestis*, Thessaly's King Admetus is allowed to escape his death by having another die in his place. When his wife, Alcestis, offers to die for him, Admetus agrees to her sacrifice. Later in the play Herakles rescues Alcestis from Thanatos, the god of death, and brings her back to her husband.

INDEX OF TITLES AND FIRST LINES

A rainy country this, that I am monarch of,—, 111
A wagon stopped before the house; she heard, 55
Admetus, from my marrow's core I do, 212
Ælfrida's Song, 97
Afternoon on a Hill, 18
Ah, cannot the curled shoots of the larkspur that you loved so, 151
Ah, drink again, 67
Alas for Man, so stealthily betrayed, 164
All I could see from where I stood, 3
All this was long ago, but I do not forget, 113
Alms, 30
And is indeed truth beauty?—at the cost, 210
And must I then, indeed, Pain, live with you, 213
And what are you that, wanting you, 26
And you as well must die, belovèd dust, 37
ARIA DA CAPO, 73
Armenonville, 199
As men have loved their lovers in times past, 154
As to some lovely temple, tenantless, 38
Autumn Chant, 39

Ballad of the Harp-Weaver, The, 41
Before this cooling planet shall be cold, 156
Believe, if ever the bridges of this town, 135

Betrothal, The, 40
Black hair you'd say she had, or rather, 204
Bluebeard, 22
Borage, forage for bees, 207
Boys and girls that held her dear, 33
Buck in the Snow, The, 65
BUCK IN THE SNOW, THE, from, 63
By the lake at Armenonville in the Bois de Boulogne, 199

Calm was Half-Moon Bay; we lay at anchor there, 200
Childhood is not from birth to a certain age and at a certain age, 148
Childhood is the Kingdom Where Nobody Dies, 148
Clearly my ruined garden as it stood, 134
Conscientious Objector, 155
CONVERSATION AT MIDNIGHT, from, 166
Cretaceous bird, your giant claw no lime, 157
Cut if you will, with Sleep's dull knife, 25
Czecho-Slovakia, 178

Daphne, 25
Death devours all lovely things, 30
Desolation Dreamed Of, 152
Desolation dreamed of, though not accomplished, 152
Dirge, 33
Dirge Without Music, 66
Dream of Saba, 200

Ebb, 32
Eclipse of the Sun Is Predicted, An, 189
Eel-Grass, 28
Elegy, 34
Elegy Before Death, 28
Epitaph, 33
Epitaph for the Race of Man, 156
Euclid alone has looked on Beauty bare, 52
Even in the moment of our earliest kiss, 140
Even you, Sweet Basil: even you, 206
Evening on Lesbos, 65

Fang, The, 105
FATAL INTERVIEW, 117
Feast, 40

Felicity of Grief!—even Death being kind, 213
FEW FIGS FROM THISTLES, A, from, 23
First Fig, 23
FLOWERS OF EVIL, from, 105
"*Fontaine, Je Ne Boirai Pas De Ton Eau!*", 177
For this your mother sweated in the cold, 68
For Warmth Alone, for Shelter Only, 204
For warmth alone, for shelter only, 204
From the wan dream that was her waking day, 59

Gazing upon him now, severe and dead, 61
"*Gentlemen Cry, Peace!*", 190
Gone in good sooth you are: not even in dream, 127
Grown-up, 25

Had I known that you were going, 47
HARP-WEAVER AND OTHER POEMS, THE, from, 39
He heard the coughing tiger in the night, 159
He woke in terror to a sky more bright, 160
Heap not on this mound, 33
Hearing your words, and not a word among them, 135
Heart, have no pity on this house of bone, 131
Here dock and tare, 147
Here is a wound that never will heal, I know, 49
Here lies, and none to mourn him but the sea, 165
Him not the golden fang of furious heaven, 163
His heatless room the watcher of the stars, 162
How healthily their feet upon the floor, 51
How shall I know, unless I go, 24
HUNTSMAN, WHAT QUARRY?, from, 174
Hyacinth, 47

I am in love with him to whom a hyacinth is dearer, 47
I am not resigned to the shutting away of loving hearts in the hard
    ground, 66
I, being born a woman and distressed, 50
I cannot but remember, 19
I drank at every vine, 40
I dreamed I moved among the Elysian fields, 124
I know I might have lived in such a way, 177
I know my mind and I have made my choice, 139

I know the face of Falsehood and her tongue, 128
I know what my heart is like, 32
I looked in my heart while the wild swans went over, 38
I must not die of pity; I must live, 191
I never was one to go to war against the weather, against the conditions, 189
I said in the beginning, did I not?—, 137
I said, seeing how the winter gale increased, 123
I shall die, but that is all that I shall do for Death, 155
I shall forget you presently, my dear, 27
I think I should have loved you presently, 26
I too beneath your moon, almighty Sex, 187
I will be the gladdest thing, 18
I will put Chaos into fourteen lines, 212
If I die solvent—die, that is to say, 214
If I should learn, in some quite casual way, 21
If in the years to come you should recall, 142
If there were balm in Gilead, I would go, 178
If to be left were to be left alone, 139
In the Grave No Flower, 147
Inland, 31
Interim, 10
Invitation to the Voyage, 108
It came into her mind, seeing how the snow, 58
It is the fashion now to wave aside, 211

King of the Rainy Country, The, 111
KING'S HENCHMAN, THE, from, 97

Late January, 111
Let them bury your big eyes, 34
Let us be circumspect, surrounded as we are, 180
Lethe, 67
Look how the bittersweet with lazy muscle moves aside, 207
Love is not all: it is not meat nor drink, 132
Love is not blind. I see with single eye, 48
Love me no more, now let the god depart, 136
Love Scene, 99

Make bright the arrows, 189
MAKE BRIGHT THE ARROWS, from, 189
Memorial to D. C., from, 33
Memory, A, 113

Midnight Oil, 25
MINE THE HARVEST, from, 195
Mists and Rains, 112
Moon, that against the lintel of the west, 130
Most wicked words!—forbear to speak them out, 134
MURDER OF LIDICE, THE, from, 192
My candle burns at both ends, 23
My heart is what it was before, 30
My most distinguished guest and learnèd friend, 126
My worship from this hour the Sparrow-Drawn, 124

Nay, learnèd doctor, these fine leeches fresh, 118
Never May the Fruit Be Plucked, 46
Never, never may the fruit be plucked from the bough, 46
Night is my sister, and how deep in love, 120
No hawk hangs over in this air, 174
No lack of counsel from the shrewd and wise, 118
No man that's worthy of the name, 105
No matter what I say, 28
Not in a silver casket cool with pearls, 122
Not only love plus awful grief, 188
Not over-kind nor over-quick in study, 57
Not So Far as the Forest, 174
Not that it matters, not that my heart's cry, 69
Not, to me, less lavish—though my dreams have been splendid, 209
Nothing could stand, 206
Now by the path I climbed, I journey back, 141
Now by this moon, before this moon shall wane, 127
Now forth to meadow as the farmer goes, 162
Now goes under, and I watch it go under, the sun, 64
Now sets his foot upon the eastern sill, 163
Now that the west is washed of clouds and clear, 186
Now the autumn shudders, 39

O ailing Love, compose your struggling wing!, 138
O Earth, unhappy planet born to die, 158
O ends of autumns, winters, springtimes deep in mud, 112
Observe how Miyanoshita cracked in two, 160
Of all that ever in extreme disease, 119
Oh, come, my lad, or go, my lad, 40
Oh, sleep forever in the Latmian cave, 143
Oh, what a shining town were Death, 147
Old Servant, The, 110

Olympian gods, mark now my bedside lamp, 122
On the Wide Heath, 153
On the wide heath at evening overtaken, 153
Once more into my arid days like dew, 36
One way there was of muting in the mind, 56
Only the diamond and the diamond's dust, 164
Only until this cigarette is ended, 35

Parisian Dream, 106
Passer Mortuus Est, 30
People that build their houses inland, 31
Peril upon the paths of this desire, 129
Philosopher, The, 26
Pierrot, a macaroon! I cannot *live* without a macaroon!, 73
Pity me not because the light of day, 48
Pluviose, hating all that lives, and loathing me, 111

Ragged Island, 196
Recuerdo, 23
Renascence, 3
Renascence and Other Poems, from, 3

Safe upon the solid rock the ugly houses stand, 23
Second April, from, 28
Second Fig, 23
See where Capella with her golden kids, 159
Seeing how I love you utterly, 182
Set the foot down with distrust upon the crust of the world—it is
    thin, 179
Shall I be prisoner till my pulses stop, 125
She filled her arms with wood, and set her chin, 54
She had a horror he would die at night, 60
She had forgotten how the August night, 58
She is neither pink nor pale, 18
She let them leave their jellies at the door, 56
Shelter this candle from the wind, 63
Since I cannot persuade you from this mood, 119
Since of no creature living the last breath, 123
Small Hands, Relinquish All, 195
Small hands, relinquish all, 195
Snow Storm, The, 174
So she came back into his house again, 53

Solid Sprite Who Stands Alone, The, 150
"Son," said my mother, 41
Sonnet, 152
Sonnet in Dialectic, 210
Sonnets from an Ungrafted Tree, 53
Sorrowful dreams remembered after waking, 133
Spring in the Garden, 151
Steepletop, 206
Strange thing that I, by nature nothing prone, 121
Summer, be seen no more within this wood, 138
Sweet love, sweet thorn, when lightly to my heart, 125
Sweeter was loss than silver coins to spend, 161

Tenderly, in those times, as though she fed, 59
That chill is in the air, 174
That marvellous landscape of my dream—, 106
The broken dike, the levee washed away, 161
The courage that my mother had, 199
The doctor asked her what she wanted done, 61
The heart once broken is a heart no more, 142
The last white sawdust on the floor was grown, 53
The mind thrust out of doors, 172
The room is full of you!—As I came in, 10
The servant that we had, you were so jealous of, 110
The solid sprite who stands alone, 150
The white bark writhed and sputtered like a fish, 54
Then cautiously she pushed the cellar door, 55
There is a well into whose bottomless eye, 141
There is no Peace; had we again the choice, 190
There, there where those black spruces crowd, 196
There was upon the sill a pencil mark, 60
There will be rose and rhododendron, 28
They marched them out to the public square, 192
Think not, nor for a moment let your mind, 126
Think, would it not be, 108
This beast that rends me in the sight of all, 117
This door you might not open, and you did, 22
This Dusky Faith, 181
Those hours when happy hours were my estate, 209
Thou famished grave, I will not fill thee yet, 187
Thou—knowest thou aught of love, and how it taketh a man?, 99
Thus are our altars polluted; nor may we flee. The walls are strong, 166

Time cannot break the bird's wing from the bird, 182
Time does not bring relief; you all have lied, 20
Time, that is pleased to lengthen out the day, 133
Time, that renews the tissues of this frame, 152
To a Friend Estranged from Me, 64
To a Young Poet, 182
To Elinor Wylie, 182
To Inez Milholland, 68
To Jesus on His Birthday, 68
To One Who Might Have Borne a Message, 47
To the Not Impossible Him, 24
To the Wife of a Sick Friend, 63
To whom the house of Montagu, 197
Tranquility at length, when autumn comes, 210
True Encounter, The, 178
Twice having seen your shingled-heads adorable, 65
Two Sonnets in Memory, 154
Two Voices, 180

Underground System, 179
Upon this marble bust that is not I, 68

Valentine, 147

Was it for this I uttered prayers, 25
We were very tired, we were very merry—, 23
Weeds, 29
Well, I have lost you; and I lost you fairly, 140
What lips my lips have kissed, and where, and why, 51
What thing is this that, built of salt and lime, 117
When Death was young and bleaching bones were few, 157
When I too long have looked upon your face, 36
When Man is gone and only gods remain, 158
When the Year Grows Old, 19
When we are old and these rejoicing veins, 131
When we that wore the myrtle wear the dust, 132
When you are dead, and your disturbing eyes, 121
Where can the heart be hidden in the ground, 155
Whereas at morning in a jeweled crown, 128
White sky, over the hemlocks bowed with snow, 65
White with daisies and red with sorrel, 29
White-thorn and black-thorn, 97

Why do you follow me?—, 25
Why, then, weep not, 181
Wild Swans, 38
WINE FROM THESE GRAPES, from, 147
Witch-Wife, 18
"Wolf!" cried my cunning heart, 178
Women have loved before as I love now, 129

Yet in an hour to come, disdainful dust, 120
You loved me not at all, but let it go, 137
You say: "Since life is cruel enough at best;", 136
Your face is like a chamber where a king, 50

AMERICAN POETS PROJECT

1. **EDNA ST. VINCENT MILLAY** / J. D. McClatchy, editor

2. **POETS OF WORLD WAR II** / Harvey Shapiro, editor

3. **KARL SHAPIRO** / John Updike, editor

4. **WALT WHITMAN** / Harold Bloom, editor

5. **EDGAR ALLAN POE** / Richard Wilbur, editor

6. **YVOR WINTERS** / Thom Gunn, editor

7. **AMERICAN WITS** / John Hollander, editor

8. **KENNETH FEARING** / Robert Polito, editor

9. **MURIEL RUKEYSER** / Adrienne Rich, editor

10. **JOHN GREENLEAF WHITTIER** / Brenda Wineapple, editor

11. **JOHN BERRYMAN** / Kevin Young, editor

12. **AMY LOWELL** / Honor Moore, editor

13. **WILLIAM CARLOS WILLIAMS** / Robert Pinsky, editor

14. **POETS OF THE CIVIL WAR** / J. D. McClatchy, editor

15. **THEODORE ROETHKE** / Edward Hirsch, editor

16. **EMMA LAZARUS** / John Hollander, editor

17. **SAMUEL MENASHE** / Christopher Ricks, editor

18. **EDITH WHARTON** / Louis Auchincloss, editor

19. **GWENDOLYN BROOKS** / Elizabeth Alexander, editor

20. **A. R. AMMONS** / David Lehman, editor

21. **COLE PORTER** / Robert Kimball, editor

22. **LOUIS ZUKOFSKY** / Charles Bernstein, editor

23. **CARL SANDBURG** / Paul Berman, editor

24. **KENNETH KOCH** / Ron Padgett, editor

25. **AMERICAN SONNETS** / David Bromwich, editor

26. **ANNE STEVENSON** / Andrew Motion, editor

27. **JAMES AGEE** / Andrew Hudgins, editor

28. **POEMS FROM THE WOMEN'S MOVEMENT** / Honor Moore, editor

29. **IRA GERSHWIN** / Robert Kimball, editor

30. **STEPHEN FOSTER & CO.** / Ken Emerson, editor

31. **COUNTEE CULLEN** / Major Jackson, editor

32. **STEPHEN CRANE** / Christopher Benfey, editor